T0065436

LAURA KLINE

Happy Dance

An experimental journey to greater health and stability through mindful movement and contact improvisation

BALBOA.PRESS

A DIVISION OF HAY HOUSE

Balboa Press books may be ordered through booksellers or by contacting:

Balboa Press
A Division of Hay House
1663 Liberty Drive
Bloomington, IN 47403
www.balboapress.com
844-682-1282

Print information available on the last page.

ISBN: 978-1-9822-5823-8 (sc)
ISBN: 978-1-9822-5824-5 (e)

Balboa Press rev. date: 11/18/2020

Dedication

This book is dedicated to my loving partner and
Sakura, our kitty. You are my world.

Acknowledgements

I would like to express my heartfelt gratitude to my dance teachers, Jean, Susie, and Maya, for their extreme dedication and talent to teaching the practice of dance, especially contact improvisation and 5Rhythms®. This book wouldn't be possible without your unyielding guidance, patience, compassion, wisdom, grace, and kindness. You know who you are. I would also like to acknowledge the special and talented dance teachers, choreographers, researchers, and dancers who paved the way for unforgettable teachers like you to graciously pass on your knowledge to eager students like me. I didn't get a chance to meet them personally, or study with them, like you might have, but indirectly, I am indebted to Steve Paxton and Nancy Stark Smith and so many others for their inspirational dance research in contact improvisation, and to Gabrielle Roth, for creating 5Rhythms.

I would also like to thank my family, friends, colleagues, and students for their continual support during this experimental, personal journey. Many of you know how much effort it took for me to practice each day, and then attempt to put into coherent words, and drawings, my thoughts and emotions, especially during the onset of the COVID-19 pandemic. My partner has greatly supported me through this entire process, and I'm so lucky to have her in my life. Lastly, I would like to thank Yen Ellis and the entire team at Balboa Press for believing in my story—and doing all those seemingly tiny, but hugely important, things necessary to publish this book.

Preface

After three-and-a-half months of joining an enthusiastic group of students and their talented teacher in a contact improvisation dance class at my university, as part of my research for my upcoming novel about two lesbian dancers who fall in love, I'd written 220 pages of the manuscript over a two-year period and found out something vital was missing. There were no dance scenes in the book! Aside from a few awkward attempts to describe the protagonists dancing salsa in the Mission District of San Francisco—more miss than hit—I had no idea what I was writing about.

I figured this out in 2019, while meditating with a group of women at a silent retreat on a frosty January morning. Clasping a smooth stone and asking the universe for guidance, the idea popped into my head. How could it be that I'd spent two years of my life writing a full-length novel—a lesbian romance—with its intriguing plot, witty dialogue, lovely description, and unique characters in such a marvelous city such as San Francisco, yet I knew nothing about dance? The premise of the book focused on two female dancers falling in love with each other, but I hadn't even written a page about dance. No wonder my story sounded flat. How ridiculous was that?

So, when it came time to share our thoughts at this early-morning retreat, before we vowed to remain silent for the rest of the day, I cleared my voice and tentatively raised my hand. Avoiding everyone's eyes, I shared that I was a writer, but I had no idea what I was doing. Sure, I'd published two novels with a mid-sized publisher, and I'd promised to deliver a third. I'd even taught creative writing for seven years... but obviously, my research skills left plenty to be desired.

Luckily, I'd signed up for this silent retreat to become enlightened. After my face reddened and I'd shared my predicament, one of the group members announced she had an idea. She scrawled something on a piece of paper and left it on the table for me, next to a nifty assortment of herbal tea, hard-boiled eggs, and a basket of mini banana muffins. During our silent snack break, I found the scrap of paper and stuffed it in my jacket. She'd written '5Rhythms' on it. I didn't know what that was, and even though I had good intentions, I sort of forgot about it. That's what my mind does to me, sometimes. I get all these great ideas in my brain, firing off at once. I plan to do all these marvelous things, until they slip through the cracks and my mind moves on to something new and shiny, which catches all my attention, until the next fabulous idea pops into my head. I learned while I was writing this manuscript that I probably have Attention-Deficit Hyperactivity Disorder (ADHD). In any case, the support group that I recently found for adults with ADHD has helped me immensely.

Back to my story...Two months later, when I was cleaning out my jacket pockets, the paper dropped to the floor. I couldn't exactly remember what 5Rhythms was, so I googled it. That was in early March 2019. Watching videos of people dancing to cool music mesmerized me and my partner. It didn't take much nudging to convince her to sign up with me for Maya's class. After an exhilarating first afternoon of dancing, we were sweaty and sore, but ready for more. So, we started dancing each week with Maya and her group of faithful followers. Being in this tight knit yet very inclusive group opened our eyes to possibilities, with our bodies, our minds, and connecting with others. Through weekly dance sessions, synching our spontaneous movement to the five rhythms matched to various types of music, I realized that dancing was not only what I needed to add to my manuscript, I craved it for my physical and mental well-being.

After nine months of religiously dancing the 5Rhythms with Maya and her group, with several intensive 5Rhythms workshops— some that had us dancing eight hours a day, for two or three days at a time—I knew I couldn't give up dancing. It had bitten me like a fierce bug, piercing my skin, ripping a neat chunk from my flesh. (Not literally, but that's how I felt.) I needed more. Like a thirsty bee, I craved our weekly dance sessions. Buzzing through the air, spinning, twirling, rolling, dancing to my own groove, shaking my hips, sweating until my T-shirt and short hair glistened like soggy rags, I couldn't get enough of 5Rhythms and moving on the dance floor with our weekly group.

I thrived on the diverse sequences of world music that bathed us in our movement, letting it stream through our veins, feeling it as it held us, centering at the core of our bodies, and hearts. This discovery of movement grounded me, restoring all my energy, even when I was so beat, all I wanted to do was collapse on the sofa with a novel and steamy mug of hot cocoa. My partner and I were learning to take refuge in this unprompted, modern form of dance, relishing it, recognizing that it had become our sanctuary, our special kind of worship—a weekly gift to help us practice how to refresh and revitalize ourselves.

Stepping back, then stepping in. I learned to navigate my emotions and body through 5Rhythms. Was I in midlife crisis? I didn't know, and I didn't care.

So, when the opportunity came up to join this contact improvisation dance class at my university, in Spring 2020, I took a calculated chance—not without plenty of reservations—to find out what I was really made of. In the dance world, contact improvisation is known for being a high-risk activity. Perhaps that wasn't the most logical choice for someone of my age, especially since I had always been accident prone, and I had several physical conditions that were supposed to prevent me from doing any kind of contact sport. But I'd never been very logical or pragmatic. Instead, I followed my intuition and, of course, signed up for the course.

What I carefully recorded in this journal was intended to become my specific research for the romance novel that I had been writing—and then stopped, so that I could delve further into the subject of dance. How was I to know that a pandemic would hit halfway through the semester, forcing us to stay at home and study dance remotely through Zoom?

In the following pages, this dance journal describes my experimental journey toward greater health and stability through mindful movement and contact improvisation. It records my subjective experience—and evidence—of a momentous transformation that I felt in the relationship between my body, mind, and spirit. It illustrates how dance—specifically, what I call the Happy Dance—has lifted me up, providing me with a safe space to traverse certain unexpected rocky roads, pebbled with injury and stress. Dancing every day—even for five short minutes while standing still in pure silence—has created a youthful buoyancy in my musculoskeletal system, lubricating my achy joints, giving me a certain bounce when I tread barefoot into the kitchen. It's helped me find increasing mental and physical stability and allowed me to thrive despite living for months on end in cramped quarters with my partner and cat, alongside our boisterous neighbors.

This journal explains a personal and detailed revelation of movement and connection, through dance. Day 1 starts out with my reflection of my impressions on the first day of our contact improvisation class. Even though I was terribly nervous about embarking on this new journey, I realized what a tremendous opportunity this dance class could bring to the protagonists in my novel. I would finally help them develop into real dancers on the page. Little did I suspect just how impactful this class, along with my 5Rhythms dance sessions and workshops, would become to my personal growth and worldview. I never would have guessed how it could alter my perceptions of life, sustain my daily existence, force me to slow down and 'experience the intense flavor of each moment,' and even enhance my survival skills.

Without realizing it, I had become the protagonist of my own book—this journal.

When the COVID-19 pandemic hit, my day-to-day written reflections broadened to include noisy neighbors, walls closing in on me, my partner, and our cat during the sudden stay-at-home order, struggles with teaching emergency remote learning classes, loss of sleep, minor bouts of hypochondria, weight loss, lack of protein due to irregular food deliveries, etc.

In summary, doing the Happy Dance as a daily practice has given me a more balanced existence. It has pried off the rust and dust that had gradually accumulated in my muscles, joints, and bones after fifty-five years on this planet. It has lubricated squeaky doors hinged to my body and mind, which had become encrusted through decades of overuse and neglect. It has taught me how to search for safety and meaningful connections with others in the midst of a global pandemic.

In this journal, I have attempted to remain authentic and true to my own experience, through somatic awareness and discovery, mindfulness of movement, facing personal injury, then healing, feeling extreme lightness of being, etc. Nearly all of the names and identifying details that I recorded in my journal have been changed in this book to protect people's identity.

At the end of our course, after three-and-a-half months of studying contact improvisation and the technical qualities of dance from a talented teacher, artist, and choreographer, along with her direct supervisor and a caring group of diverse college students, I submitted my own definition of contact improvisation for my final reflection (see the end of this book).

Now that I have published this manuscript, I have no idea if anyone will be interested in reading it, besides my immediate family and close friends, and hopefully, my dance teachers. But secretly, I wish that one day, it might land in the hands of at least one curious reader who will discover, like me—even at middle-age—the tremendous healing and unexpected wonders of dance. By reading the pages of this journal, and shedding your shoes to try the Happy Dance, perhaps you too will forge a deeper connection to yourself and all living beings on Earth.

To conclude, perhaps this would be an appropriate place to mention that readers should consider consulting with their physicians before trying any of the practices in this book, especially the high-risk practices. As the author, my intent is not to provide medical advice nor treat physical or mental health issues. Therefore, in the event that you utilize any of the information or try any of the techniques described in this book, neither the author nor the publisher shall be held responsible for your actions.

Happy reading!

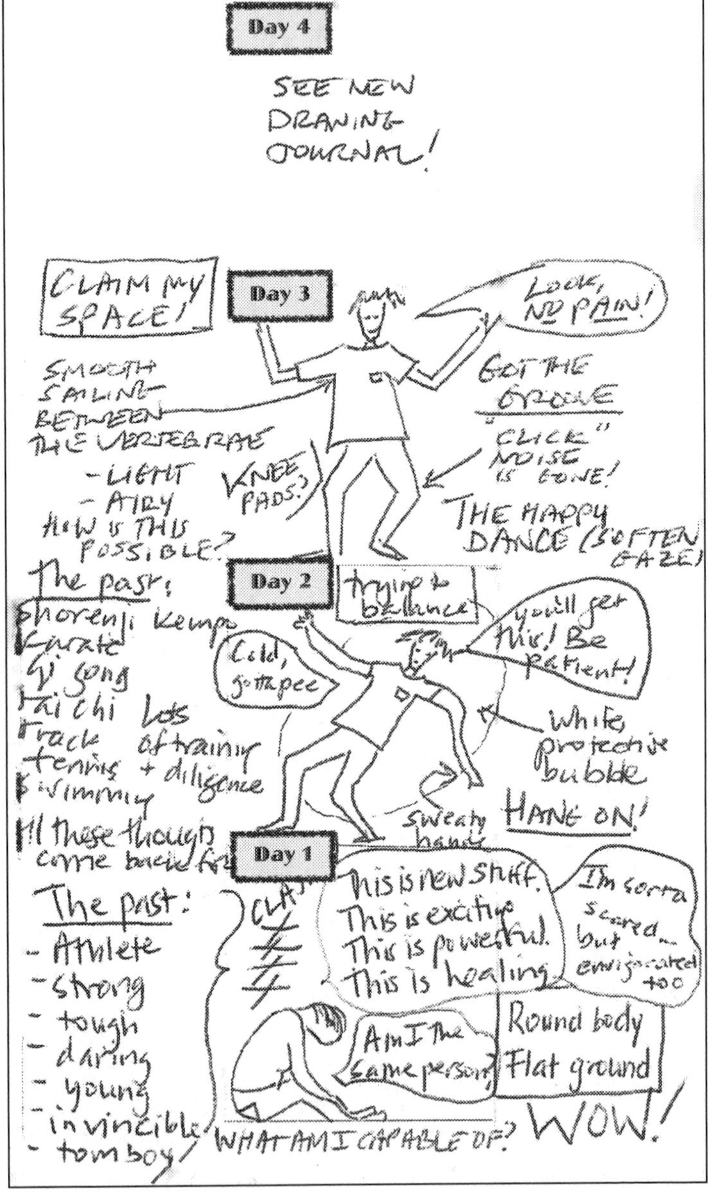
Day 4
SEE NEW DRAWING JOURNAL!
CLAIM MY SPACE!
Day 3
Look, NO PAIN!
SMOOTH SAILING BETWEEN THE VERTEBRAE
- LIGHT
- AIRY
HOW IS THIS POSSIBLE?
KNEE PADS?
GOT THE GROOVE
"CLICK" NOISE IS GONE!
THE HAPPY DANCE (SOFTEN GAZE)
The past:
Shorenji Kempo
Karate
Qi gong
Tai Chi
Track
tennis
swimming
Lots of training + diligence
Day 2
trying to balance
Cold, gotta pee
you'll get this! Be patient!
White protective bubble
HANG ON!
Sweaty hands
Day 1
The past:
- Athlete
- strong
- tough
- daring
- young
- invincible
- tomboy
This is new stuff.
This is exciting
This is powerful.
This is healing
I'm sorta scared... but envigorated too
Am I the same person?
Round body
Flat ground
WHAT AM I CAPABLE OF?
WOW!

Day 4 A new exercise.
New thoughts.
New sensations.
BUTTING HEADS (in a soft yet firm way)

Where are those knee pads?

3 joints
1 bone
2 bones
3 joints
1 bone
2 bones

What if someone sees us?

Feeling the floor with my breath, and feeling the skin bones and flesh of the others with my feet. We are round, the floor is flat. Twisting, turning, forgetting to breathe, forgetting to turn and look at the other. Learning to dance as one. Oiling the joints. Learning physiology in movement. Quiet stillness & smooth movement through space.

OM~ OM~

STILLNESS & SILENCE

Time stops

Sketchbook, Days 1 to 4

January 23rd, 2020, Thursday, Day 1

I have so much to write I could fill this entire journal in one entry today. But I'll wait, because I have to get to my somatics class and eat. I've been taking somatics for a little over a year, and when I looked it up online, a few websites basically said that it helps practitioners become more aware of their bodies and how they function. That's totally true. I feel like it's related to dance, but it's not quite the same. It's like going back in time, reuniting ourselves with our younger bodies, making them more flexible and easier to move—like being a kid again.

I did a drawing about what it was like to realize all this stuff coming up from the past yesterday at our first contact improvisation class with Jean. It was a wonderful introduction, full of meaning, care, and compassion, yet it drove me into my past in so many unexpected ways. I had never figured out that we were round bodies in a flat world, on a flat surface—the ground. This concept makes a lot of sense and explains why it's hard for me to sit on the ground without shifting and feeling uncomfortable for long periods of time.

The drawing reflects my thoughts, awareness, and body image of me now, as compared to the past. All of this will come out in my journal, which will help me not only flesh out the character in my next novel, who is a lot like I was thirty years ago—but it will help me realize who I am, now, where I've been in the past, with my body (soma), mind and spirit, and hopefully, where I'm headed. In a new direction, I'm sure. Staying the same is not only impossible, it's insane.

This is a tremendous opportunity for growth, introspection, and to deepen the connection to myself, to others, to the earth, and the world. I am forever indebted to Susie and Jean for allowing me to participate in this dance course. I'm so excited already!

Here is my week one journal entry, due by 10:30 am on Monday.

It's a reflective assignment where we first describe our current physical activities: I do gentle yoga once a week, I take a somatics class once a week, I dance to the 5Rhythms for two hours once a week, and sometimes on my own in the morning. I walk once or twice per day for thirty minutes and try to climb at least two big hills for aerobic exercise. I swim once or twice per week for thirteen minutes, and sometimes bike fifteen minutes on a stationary bike. I also teach at our campus, and as I carry my books, papers, lunch, etc., with me to all my classes, three days a week, it's quite a workout.

We also have to write about how touch is present in our lives. When I dance to the 5Rhythms I sometimes touch others who are open and willing to be touched. It usually happens when a guest instructor asks us to do it. I used to do a lot of ballroom dancing in college, so touch was very present. Now, it's much less, though I write about it in my latest novel, so I at least imagine doing it while I'm dancing. I touch our cat a lot (petting), and my partner (holding hands, hugging, etc.), and I give hugs to friends and handshakes to new people. The first thing I do in the morning is touch my face to wash and dry it, which wakes me up. And it also stimulates my skin. It's a ritual before meditating with my tea.

Next, Jean asked us how we think we move. I like this question a lot. I was a huge tomboy as a kid, and very athletic, so I move in a way that's not very feminine, according to our society's norms. I used to be super confident, agile, and muscular, and proud of the power that I had in my body, so I moved with my head held high and my shoulders back. Then I relocated to Europe, and then Japan, and I lost all of that confidence and power, and moved more like a woman should. Sometimes even like a scared mouse. When I worked in Brussels, Belgium, right after spending six years in Japan, the security guards thought I was British, I was so reserved, polite and humble. I was just being Japanese and avoiding eye contact by looking at the floor. Now, back in California, I try to move with confidence and agility. I'm no longer a monkey or tomboy, and dance has taught me an appreciation for soft, flowing, graceful moves as I walk, stand, sit, and move about the dance floor.

Lastly, we are supposed to describe our goals for this course, and how our identities fit in with regard to dance and movement. Well, I'd like to explore as many aspects of contact improvisation as possible, so that I can fully immerse myself in all the learning in our group, with Jean's guidance, and by listening to my own body's needs, as I interact and dance with the others in class. I know I have certain physical limitations (neck and knees, especially), that I have shared with Jean via email, so if she allows me to continue in the course despite these concerns, I will be extra careful not to get injured or allow my physical limitations to hinder others in the group. I hope to grow and expand my knowledge and awareness about the mind-body-spirit connection, space, and physics through movement. And I've never done that kind of improvisation, only speaking improv, part-time acting, and a bit of comedy, so this new adventure on the dance floor will hopefully teach me to become more aware and conscious of myself and others, and our interactions through movement and stillness.

I teach mindfulness and gentle yoga, and I used to teach martial arts, too, so I'm aware of a lot through movement and bodily sensations, but this is all something new to me and I come at it with a very open mind. I used to do "Barefoot boogie" on Sunday nights in San Francisco at 24th and Mission, where we danced and touched each other spontaneously, so perhaps part of that was improv? With regard to my body/identity, I hope to be much stronger and more confident in my body through the work in this course, kind of like when I was a young athlete, or when I did lots of martial arts. I look forward to carrying myself with more self-assurance, grace, and awareness of the space and others around me.

Moreover, as a queer person and an activist—I write LGBTQ+ fiction and talk a lot about LGBTQ+ inclusivity in literature and in society—I hope that this research that I'm doing for myself, through movement, dance, and contact improv, and for my characters, will show up in the pages of my next novel in an authentic way. The two protagonists are queer, and I hope to do them justice—and the dance world justice—by authentically representing them as dancers, and as queer, wonderful, and fully alive human beings. They are featured in my book so that when it comes out, and once I've researched contact improvisation through this course, people will read it and learn about the qualities of dance and the qualities of people who are queer. Neither should be hidden; both dance and queerness should be celebrated worldwide, in my opinion, and if I have to dance at my book signings and author events at libraries, bookstores, and writer's festivals to demonstrate this, I will be delighted and honored to do so. This is how I imagine how my body might become an agent of change. Maybe I could even get a group of dancers to make a video with me to make an even bigger impact, and we could go on the Ellen show to be broadcast to the world!

January 27, 2020, Monday, Day 2

I realized after our dance class today that I didn't know the prompt for this week's journal entry. I missed the last five minutes of class, so I could change and make it to my own classroom on time. I had forty-three students waiting for me to do mindfulness with them at the start of class, five minutes of what I call 'settling-in,' and today we had a guest speaker. It was kind of stressful, to get there in an incognito fashion. I haven't told anyone I was taking this course, except my partner, my aunt, and my immediate family. I certainly haven't told my students!

Once again, I got a lot out of today's dance class. I had certain apprehensions, and even some fear, before we started moving. I wondered: *Will we warm up? Should I have warmed up? Will I get too cold with bare feet?* And I worried about sweating and then going to my next two classes, office hours, teaching another class, and then volunteering at our mindfulness class, for three hours tonight, straight after my last class. But when we sat in the circle and Jean started talking in such a calm way, and when the students—including me—noticeably relaxed on the floor, I knew it would all work out. She has a very calm, patient demeanor that lends itself perfectly to teaching dance, and contact improvisation (C.I.). She puts everyone at ease and no question is considered 'stupid.' That's a relief.

I could go on and on about the pedagogy in our opening circle; my academic research is on contemplative pedagogy, and mindfulness, but for the purpose of this journal, I'll write about what I learned through movement, and non-movement, today. I'll do that right after I teach my last class and assistant teach tonight! By then, maybe I'll know the prompt, if there is one.

January 29, 2020, Wednesday, Day 3

I know now that there aren't specific prompts for this journal. I can just do free writing and perhaps back up my reflections with the extensive reading list Jean gave us in the syllabus. That reading list is amazing. I never knew dance had so many ties to social justice and identity work. I should have guessed this, but I didn't. It's never too late to learn!

Yesterday in class I really felt the gravity pulling me down at certain points in our movement, and when we stopped. It was cool to notice this. And I felt like I moved slower and more carefully than most of the students, who were much younger than me. I wondered if I would have responded differently to Jean's instructions to move if I were their age. Probably so. Noticing gravity pulling me down gave my body a deep, heavy feeling, like I was really connected to the ground and earth. At other times, I felt lighter. Warming up by moving and taking up space in our own creative ways was a great way to warm up our muscles and play. I should do that every day.

It reminded me of the *Flowing* part of our 5Rhythms dance practice, which I do every Sunday and, sometimes, at home alone in my living room. *Flowing* is my favorite part of 5Rhythms, usually. But I do like to let out steam with *Staccato* and *Chaos* as well, if I'm in the mood. A big difference is that in our contact improvisation class, we're moving in silence, not to music. I kind of like dancing without music. I can feel more what's going on inside my body.

It was interesting walking and sharing our experiences with another student as we walked. I was next to the student who had injured her foot, so she and I walked slowly, and carefully, as we exchanged thoughts. Then we did this exercise about space and energy, putting our hands near each other's; then touching (skin), then muscles, then bone (skeleton), which I thought was amazing. I have a vague recollection of doing something similar in my *qi gong* martial arts courses in Brussels, way back when, playing with the

Laura Kline

energy (*qi*) of each other, and we even threw people, through people standing back-to-back in a line, using this *qi*. I found it fascinating then, and this time it was, too.

We closed our eyes and felt, through hand-to-hand contact, all of this—all of the self, and the other person, planted firmly on the ground. I didn't want to take her off-balance, because she was in a booty for her injured foot, but she held strong and so I let that thought go. A lot of dance, and mindfulness, means letting go of things, and thoughts, that don't serve us. It teaches us acceptance, non-striving, non-judgment, etc. So, I let that go, but I did notice that both of our hands were getting really warm (hers, to the touch, and mine), and later, sweaty. I wondered if I was the one sweating, or her, or both of us. Then again, I decided to let that thought go, because I couldn't do anything about it. I wasn't going to wipe my hands on my pants during this exercise; that would be rude, I guess.

A lot of self-awareness and self-consciousness came into my mind during this particular exercise. I also wondered if she thought it was weird or uncomfortable to do this with someone much older than her, who most likely taught on campus, instead of studied. Apparently, as I was leaving the group, Jean had told the class that I taught university courses.

Self-awareness, self-consciousness, and doubt fill my mind a lot, it seems, and this class will let me realize just how much this is so. Perhaps it will help fill me with confidence again as I become more empowered, balanced, and centered in my body. I can already feel a difference in the way I stand, sit, and walk. There's more purposeful consciousness in my stance, where and how I move my muscles, and in my gait.

It is as if I'm learning to occupy all of the cells of my body again, like when I was first born, which is a tremendous gift, because this is my birthright. I have a little bit of dyslexia, like my brother, and it comes out sometimes when I write. For some reason, however, in this dance journal, the words seem to flow, happily, so I'm not experiencing so many issues with putting down my thoughts and words in an orderly fashion. I think it's because I'm learning to flow with my body, and my mind, at last! So that makes it easier to express my feelings on paper.

I noticed again that we didn't have music on during our class. I wonder if we'll have music later on, like we do in 5Rhythms. I think it's kind of neat that we don't have sounds and vibrations to interfere with our learning, actually. Sometimes, in 5Rhythms, I get really distracted by the music and I don't feel as much awareness in my body and movement.

I also noticed that I was a bit afraid of dancing too close to the more active students in the course. I was afraid of getting hurt. Perhaps this minor fear will lessen or go away as I gain more confidence in the strength of my body, and as I get to know all the students on a more intimate basis. Because dancing, moving, and sharing space with others is an intimate thing, no matter how you look at it. I can feel the room; I can feel others, their emotions and their energy. That's a gift I've always had. I'll try to use it in this class, so I can let go of fears that no longer serve me.

January 29th, 2020, Wednesday
(continued reflection)

Even though I was afraid of being hurt, afraid of being late to my own class afterwards, afraid of what would happen to my muscles if I didn't warm up like I usually do: ankle, knee, and hip rotations, stretching, etc., and warm down in the same way, I did it. I made it through the entire class and went on to teach and it all worked out. My knees were sore afterwards; that's what happens when I don't warm up and warm down a lot, but I'll figure out a way to warm up first. Maybe, I can do it in my office, which isn't far from the dance class, luckily. And I can be overly active and bouncy as I teach for the next two hours afterwards, to stretch my muscles. ☺

I also put a tube of arnica—a miraculous healing herb in gel form that helps prevent bruising and injuries—in my office drawer to put on my knees and other body parts in case of stress or injury to my muscles. That served me well in volleyball. I was on the second-to-highest national team in Belgium, but I was the worst player by far, with no formal training. They used to say, "Do we want to win this match, or do we want to let Laura play?" That's sort of a theme in my life, doing things without proper training. I was also a graphic artist and designer in San Francisco with no real training. I invented myself and started a graphic design business at age twenty-one. And volleyball, martial arts, interpretation, translation, etc., they all sort of fell into my life because I wanted to do those things with passion. Teaching, photos, writing, and filmmaking, too. Now, it's dance. I'm bitten by the dance bug and we'll see where it takes and shakes me.

It's 4:30am and I couldn't sleep, so I made myself a cup of hot cocoa and I'm writing with sleepy eyes and shaky fingers. I worried about getting too sweaty in class or having to pee. During the body scan at the start of class, I didn't have my sweater on, and my muscles cooled down. I was afraid of catching a cold, lying on the floor in a T-shirt and bare feet. After twenty minutes of agonizing over the fact that I was getting colder and colder, like a corpse, despite enjoying the practice, I finally decided to get up and put on my sweater. I didn't know if Jean would notice, or care, but the impulse was eating away at my mind and I had to do it. Felt much better, afterwards.

I'd done the body scan, like I do most days, already that morning, but I'm always immobile under a blanket with plenty of clothes, lying on my sofa or bed. I close my eyes and let my mind concentrate really slowly over each body part, starting with my right big toe, all the way up to the top of my skull. So, moving gently in the dance studio, surrounded by coolness, with Jean's guidance, was quite a novel experience. But then I had to go to the restroom. Usually, when I'm teaching mindfulness or dancing, I don't have this problem. It's like I can ignore it because I'm so happy to be doing what I'm doing. I'm 100% engrossed in the moment. But on Monday, I couldn't stand it any longer, so I went. And the sky didn't cave in. In fact, I noticed others had the same impulse, after me.

I was energized leaving the dance floor, just like on the first day, when we went over the syllabus, even without moving at all. I left class thoroughly excited for more. To protect myself from fears of catching a cold or getting injured, during the body scan I imagined a protective white bubble around me. That helped a lot; I couldn't feel the cold anymore. It reminded me of my martial arts training in Belgium and Japan when I was in my early 30's. I practiced *shorenji kempo* (Buddhist-based kung fu from Shaolin temple in China), karate, qi gong, and tai chi. I was in bare feet then, too, in northern Japan. With bare feet and only wearing our *gi* (uniform) three to four hours per class, three times a week, with snow outside, no heating, and all the windows open, I never got sick, but boy was I cold!

I was the only foreigner in nearly all of my martial arts classes. We'd sit on our knees to meditate before class in a row on the wooden floor. A long wooden pole would hit the ground next to us, or on our shoulder, with a 'crack!' if we slumped or fell asleep. Our Sensei was kind, but very strict. I had to recite the Buddhist sutras in Japanese to get to a new level. Only when the belt gets dirty (it goes from brown to black, then it becomes white from fraying), does the student advance in Japan, not like here in the West, where novice practitioners earn colored belts. My karate training was tough in our small Japanese town, but I made it through.

So, I can do this too. This activity is much softer, more spacious, and Jean is not as scary as my Sensei in Japan, who had never trained a foreigner before, and certainly not a woman *gaijin*! I was in my 30's then, not in my 50's. It's twenty years later. While we were sitting in the opening circle on Monday, my mind also went back to my beloved track team and that time when I was nineteen in college and I got injured. I felt so much a part of the team then. Now, it also feels like I'm part of the group, even though I'm much older than the other dancers. This group is inclusive, and alive; we're very present with each other and Jean. I feel guidance, spaciousness, consciousness, and so much body awareness.

It's not like at the university where I did my undergraduate studies, where our team was forced to lift weights twice a day and run to the airport six days a week. That's what ruined my knees and made me a swimmer. Three of us became swimmers because of that coach, who won a big award for her strength-based training, yet she made it so that I could never run again. It's not like that in Jean's class, luckily. Body awareness is crucial. So is breathwork and the body scan; it's all more flexible, porous, and just as exciting as running. Perhaps even more. It's a breath of fresh air (what a cliché in a square/flat world)!

Today, we have our third class. I'm looking forward to it. My clothes are all packed since last night. That's new for me, planning so far ahead. But I don't want to be late and miss out on any moment of this course. Somehow, from deep within, I feel it's vital to my growth as a human being, and essential to my writing. The more I understand and embody dance, the easier it will get to put it down on paper and live it in my life, right? This is an investment in me, and I hope I can make a valuable contribution to the world as the fruit of my efforts. I think I'm off to a good start!

January 31st, 2020, Friday, Day 3 continued

Our class on Wednesday was a revelation. I figured out I could get there a bit early and meditate in front of a tree not far from the dance building in the courtyard. This was nice because I could shut my eyes for five minutes and get some peace and calm after my drive to campus, so when I entered the studio, I was already more poised and centered. I saw Jean and Susie, her direct supervisor, talking and doing their thing, so I was free to stretch against the wall and on the floor. I was glad to have this opportunity to stretch even though I'd walked and done gentle yoga at home in the morning.

We started in a circle. Jean asked us questions, and everyone had the chance to answer in turn. I was amazed by the students' responses. They took their time and really said some deep things. When it was my turn to describe what stood out for me the most during Monday's class, I said: "The fact that I was writing furiously in my dance journal," or something to that effect. Some students laughed a bit (I was the only one to mention my journal). It was the truth, though. I really like writing about my impressions in this journal. I even found myself frustrated this week because I needed to plan my classes and create slides, etc., when all I felt like doing was writing my thoughts in here. Luckily, I could carve out an hour today after teaching to write, despite it being a windy day and my notebook got a bit wet from someone's leftover tea. Like usual, I'm at an outdoor cafe.

The biggest revelation that I had on Wednesday was that I came to class apprehensive about my knees hurting, especially my right one, because I hurt my hip/thigh muscle pulling a box of blankets across the floor after my mindfulness class on Monday night, which made my knee click a bit on Tuesday. And yet when I left the dance class on Wednesday, I had a spring to my step that wasn't there before and *no* pain in the knees: no clicking, no pain anywhere! I was shocked, and relieved, and very, very pleased! So, I can do this!

We spent nearly two hours rolling, sliding, moving, walking backwards, twirling, etc., on the hard dance floor. I didn't have knee pads yet, and my knees are really bony. Jean showed me hers when I said that, and I was glad to see that hers are too, sort of, and she has no issues with this. Yet I wasn't in pain. I was in far less physical pain and discomfort than when I went into the class. It became a release of tension, and as I was "juicing up my joints," as she says, "three in the legs and three in the arms," I was lubricating all the tight and sticky areas of my spine. She even explained the roundness of the back and vertebrae, and it seemed like I was floating on air. I even felt the sponginess between my vertebrae expand as I walked down the halls after class—it was weird. My gait was smoother, more intentional, more mindful, and deliberate; I walked like a kid in new sneakers with lots of rubber and foam in them. I was delighted.

And on the floor, I felt a bit like a tarantula with my legs up, then down, turning and twisting like a spider, and rolling on parts of my body that I'd never dared roll on before, like my nose and eyelids! This created space, with lots of sensations all over, like an awkward massage that is painful but exciting too. I felt my joints, muscles, ligaments, and tendons bend and stretch like never before. I felt like I was getting younger, while grooving all over the place: inching along, then twirling, leaping, etc. We went through lots of playful awareness and soliciting our curiosity, like we do in mindfulness training. That makes sense, because this *is* mindfulness. It's sensory training, using all the senses together, especially those of touch. We're gaining all kinds of insight using our skin, bones, muscles, etc.

We did an exercise at the end, after we did a bit of dance, butting heads. That was interesting and I was glad a student dared to do it with me, on all fours, even though he had his cap on (in addition to Susie, who's not as afraid of me as the younger students, I imagine). When we paired up at the end to do an exercise using our hands, Susie and I were left alone, so we paired up. Jean asked us to do the 'happy dance,' then put our hands up facing the other person's, without touching. I didn't understand what she meant by the 'happy dance,' and I did it wrong because I left my eyes open. We were standing pretty close, facing each other, and trying to feel our feet through gravity by noticing how they connected to the round earth on a flat surface. It was supposed to be a grounding exercise, using conscious breathing, increasing our spatial awareness and connection to our partner through touch. And at the same time, we were supposed to try to feel the energy flowing through our partner's feet, where they connected to the floor. This practice was all done in silence, so we could *feel* all the living cells in our bodies, from the tops of our skulls to our elbow joints, to the floor of our pelvis, to the skin on our toes.

Susie said to Jean, when I told her I thought I didn't grasp the concept, to "please explain the eyes," or something like that.

Now that I read this entry, I believe she asked us to do the small dance, which was invented by Steve Paxton in 1972 when he started the practice of contact improvisation. I kept calling it the happy dance, because when I did it, it made me happy. It still does!

Jean said to look down slightly or close the eyes. Then I realized that on Monday I was supposed to do that too, and the student I'd worked with didn't come back on Wednesday. I felt self-conscious in front of Susie, who had lowered her gaze and I hadn't, until then. I kept thinking that the student probably thought I was this creep because I kept my eyes open—and on her—not knowing that this wasn't part of the 'happy dance.' So, I did the practice with Susie, starting off in a self-conscious way. Dance is really intimate; people are invited into each other's space through movement and touch. I'll learn to get a grasp of this, but it's a process.

In the past, I did lots of ballroom dance and gyrated on podiums in clubs, but this theoretical concept, this cognitive and psychological aspect of dance, blows my mind. Gravity and balance do too. I've already figured out how all this learning and practicing contact improvisation—and we're only on our third lesson—is helping me in my life. I realize it's potentially a very high-risk activity, but it's so exhilarating and fun, after reading both articles from CQ (Contact Quarterly), the magazine about contact improvisation that we had to read for Monday. Very enlightening.

I also realize it's teaching me about boundaries and my need for space, and how important it is for me to articulate this need for space, even to my partner. I've never noticed it before, but this morning she came in to brush her teeth, and I was drying my hair with a blow dryer. There's very little space in our bathroom and only one sink, unfortunately. I realized then how cramped it was, and how I wanted all the space to myself. Without noticing how I felt—how could she?—she wanted to talk, then brush her teeth. I can't believe it now, but I invited her to please leave the space. She was hurt and left in a huff while I continued to dry my hair.

This is new for us. I've never really claimed my space or quietness when I really needed it because I was rushing, I imagine, yet this morning I did. I think it's due to dancing and exploring spatial awareness and how important consent is, even if it's to share the bathroom for a few minutes. Even if the couple has been living together for years and normally gives each other all forms of respect, like us. That's why this was so surprising to me. And I held my space (ground) and didn't regret it. It was empowering. But now that I write this, I feel bad about how I acted towards her. I was unusually blunt. What I said, and how I said it, sounded quite rude.

There I stood, legs apart, feet pointed out, drying my hair. I was taking up room like Wonder Woman! Amazing. I felt more powerful than I'd felt in a long time. It's sort of scary, though, when I think about it. I'll have to be careful not to be too direct with my newfound spatial awareness, with my partner and with others.

Today and yesterday my muscles are tense and sore again, so I think I'll try to do that jumping exercise (very little jiggles of feet, legs, hands, arms, and body) that we did on Wednesday. I'm sure that exercise, coupled with rolling like a taquito/spider on the ground, is what loosened my joints, muscles and fascia, and made me feel great. I'm looking forward to Monday's class, of course, and exploring more about dance in the coming weeks. What's going to unfold/unravel next?

February 4th, 2020, Tuesday, Day 4

Yesterday, we had a great class. Once again, I learned a lot about myself, my body, and my mind. I'm quite self-conscious on the dance floor when we're asked to move amongst or against each other. I think if I were the same age as the others it would be less of an issue for me, but because I'm older—but not necessarily wiser—I imagine they'd rather hang out with each other instead of me.

So, I was happy when one, then two, then a third student did the exercise with me… where we had to slide, crawl, or move under or over the other person, who used their body to form a teepee, or tent, on the floor. I went under one girl first, then someone went under me, then I went under someone, like a worm. That was what broke the eyes—and ice—on a physical and mental level for me. It was kind of scary but exciting too.

Next, we did a lot of rolling on the floor again in various ways, learning to feel the ground with all parts of our bodies, especially the pelvis, ribs, shoulders, head, etc. Without knee pads my knees and joints were getting sore on the cold, hard surface. Finally, I got a message from Jean today that Susie will bring them for us tomorrow. That's really good news. Also, I keep bringing my dance journal to class and we haven't used it yet. I suppose it's important to bring the journal each time, in case I get injured, or arrive late, which I hope will never happen.

Towards the middle of class Jean asked everyone to pair up and I had nobody, so she asked me if I would demonstrate the next exercise with her. I said "yes," not knowing what would happen next. It's kind of exhilarating to not know what's coming, while everyone's watching. She proceeded to explain that we would be butting heads and moving around the room. She didn't exactly say that, but that's what we did. With our heads connected on top and on the sides, etc., we twisted, turned, and rotated our bodies. It was like a strange dance on the floor and in the air.

It was hard at first because I knew everyone was watching and I didn't know who was supposed to lead. I didn't want to dominate too much by initiating every turn, and I didn't want to be too passive either. The others started doing it, too, and we continued. Then she stopped to explain and check on the others. I mentioned my apprehension about leading/being led, etc., and then she explained an important detail about keeping my neck strong, as if my neck went from the back of my skull to my tailbone. I tried that, and it made it much easier on my cervical vertebrae.

During this exercise, I was feeling the floor with my breath, and feeling the skin, bones, and flesh of the other with my feet, as Jean instructed us. She reminded us that we are round, and the floor is flat. Twisting, turning, forgetting to breathe, forgetting to turn and look at the other. Learning to dance as one. We were "oiling the joints," and learning physiology in movement. Exploring quiet stillness and smooth movement through space.

At a certain point we were all dancing with one arm up and the other hand near our buttocks, with our finger resting on our tailbone—quite interesting. Both times, when I was dancing head-to-head with Jean on the floor, and when we had our fingers on our tailbones, it looked like our fingers were somewhere else—up our butts. I was worried that someone I knew, faculty, staff, or my students, might come by and snap a photo of me doing this, to show the world. "Oh well!" I decided and kept on dancing.

What's neat is that we start out each class sitting in an opening circle, all together. It's so inclusive, and I can feel the spaciousness around each of us. We are so present, it's palpable. Jean gives us gentle guidance, without reprimands. Everyone is responsible for his/her/their own health, hygiene, homework, and happiness—all the 'h's and all the other letters, too. My mind wanders, then comes back. It's such a great experience. I feel so blessed to be in this class.

I'll end this entry with another high point. Today, I went to my gentle yoga class at the YMCA for the first time in two weeks. This time, in class, instead of getting impatient or bored or wishing it were over after thirty minutes—it's a one hour and twenty-minute class—I actually enjoyed the whole thing. One hour and twenty minutes is shorter than two hours, which I'm now used to. It hurt a lot less, too. We had nice, firm mats under our knees, and I realized I was much more flexible, and stronger, when I did the sun salutations, etc. I went much farther, without pushing or forcing my body. I was gentle and patient with myself, which is new. And I was tolerant of others—even the guy whose feet always smell, and the woman with a scowl. Time seemed so precious, and it's thanks to our dance class and Jean, and me showing up!

Even though my knee and other joints still click, I feel like they're getting juiced up a lot with all this movement. I'm still surprised that we do no stretching before or after class; maybe that's what we're supposed to do at home. It's a great experience to be in this class and I'm excited already for tomorrow. I prepare my clothes for teaching and dance class the night before—something I've never done, except when I used to bike to work in Brussels. For five years nobody knew I biked eighteen kilometers per day in the rain before and after work. It's like I had a double life and now I'm doing it again at school with dance!

Day 5

JIM

ME→

HOT HANDS

FEEL THE CONNECTION

Knee pads - yeah!

WE'RE STANDING ON LIVE ANIMALS, THE EARTH IS ALIVE AND CONSCIOUS, EVER REVOLVING; WE'RE DOING THE HAPPY DANCE (SWEATY HANDS ARE OKAY!!!)
SOFT TOUCH. GENTLE PRESSURE. SENSITIVITY.

NICE GUYS ↑ WORK WITH!

PAUL

"YOU'RE TOUGH!"

I TAKE THAT AS A COMPLIMENT. MARTIAL ARTS TRAINING HAS TAUGHT ME VALUABLE LESSONS.

proud of myself ☺

STRONG

OUCH!

ME→

Be careful!

knee pads

SORE TOMORROW!
Sensitive knee joints = (ARNICA)

SQUATTING IS NOT MY FORTE

THOUGHTS! I'M SORE ALL OVER. I DNT KNOW I HAD THIS MANY MUSCLES. GOING UP AND DOWN STAIRS MORE CAREFULLY AND SLOWLY, LIKE AN OLD, CREAKY-BONED LADY. YET I'M ENERGISED AND 3 PEOPLE HAVE SAID, "WOW (WOW), YOU'RE STRONG!" IN 2 DAYS. THAT MAKES ME HAPPY, BECAUSE I'VE ALWAYS BEEN ATHLETIC + STRONG AND I LET SOME OF THAT GO THESE PAST 10 YEARS. TIME TO CLAIM MY FLEXIBILITY (MENTAL AND PHYSICAL) BACK, AND MY STRENGTH (BONES, MUSCLES, JOINTS, LIGAMENTS, ETC., EVEN SKIN!) NEW SENSATIONS COME, NEW CONCEPTS, IDEAS. MY FIELD OF VISION WIDENS AND I REALIZE IT'S LIMITLESS. TIME TO FOLLOW MY DREAMS TO FULL VITALITY!

Sketchbook, Day 5

February 7th, 2020, Friday, Day 5

I drew in my little sketchbook yesterday so I could illustrate what it was like doing the exercises with Jim and Paul on Wednesday. Over half of class time was devoted to doing these exercises, where we put our hands on the shoulders of our partner and then, doing the happy dance, we moved with them around the dance floor. Jim didn't have a partner and neither did I, so he asked me if we could work together.

I was glad to have a partner and not try this alone, and it worked out well. I was worried that he'd push too hard on my shoulders and compress my spine. With scoliosis, that's not a good thing. But I was pleasantly surprised how mindful and gentle his touch was, once he finally laid his hands on my shoulders. He didn't push or force anything when he was guiding me around. On the contrary, his touch was light, and even reassuring. It was warm, too; even through my two shirts. I tried to do the same thing: have a light, sensitive touch that wasn't too invasive or controlling. And I think it worked.

Jean said, "We're standing on live animals. The earth is alive and conscious, ever revolving." We were doing the happy dance and sweaty hands were okay. We needed to have a soft touch, with gentle pressure and sensitivity.

I know my dad, or one of my brothers, would have wanted to show his male force and would have steered me around like a ship or a marionette. I would have felt crushed and oppressed with no choice but to follow his aggressive moves. Jim's touch was as soft as a feather (another cliché), and that moved me; I realized then that not all men were overpowering jerks on a physical level.

When we did the exercise—where we had to back the other person towards the wall by placing our hands against both of theirs and pushing—it reminded me a lot of my qi gong, shorenji kempo, and karate training in Japan and Belgium. We used to line people up and throw the last person in line with solely our qi (or chi), which means energy. I was the one who destabilized and threw people the farthest, even strong policemen, so nobody wanted to be at the end of the line when it was my turn.

All we did was put our hands on the shoulders of the person in front of us, who had their hands on the person in front of them, etc. Nobody moved. I would send my chi (qi) from the earth through my feet, through my *dan tien* (belly) and into my arms and hands, which were very hot with chi (or qi). My writing of these Asian characters isn't as good as it used to be, when I was a student in Japan, studying Japanese and Chinese, Buddhism, and martial arts.

When I did that exercise with Jim, and then Paul, I'm pretty sure they were surprised at my force and strength. I tried to be gentle and calm, but that competitive edge that I was raised with, that fighting spirit taught to me by my dad—a professional athlete and my coach, unfortunately, because he broke my spirit in so many ways—came back in full force. I saw myself training with the male Police Academy in Japan, in the evenings. It was really tough. I had so many bruises from those karate classes and my shorenji kempo (kung fu) sessions that people thought I was battered at home by my non-existent husband. It was embarrassing.

So, I tried to be gentle and not overpower these men when I did the exercise with them. I only used 60% of my force and I was able to push them fully across the room and stop them when they tried to push me backwards. I gave in so they could push me, while thinking I couldn't stop them—but I could. In our society, I've been taught that men should always come out on top in sports, and I didn't want to hurt their egos. I'm older, and a woman, so I'm sure that I would have bruised their egos had I really gone full force. At least, that's what my mind was saying, but then again, they were not like most of the male figures that I had growing up—bullies. And that wasn't the point of the exercise anyway.

I like how compassion, care, consent, and respect are big parts of this course. It teaches me so much about life, humanity, and myself. My knees do hurt now, despite the knee pads. I realize that squatting is not my forte. I'm sore all over; I didn't know I had so many muscles. I'm going up and down stairs more carefully and slowly, like a creaky-boned lady. Yet I'm energized and three people have said to me, "Wow, you're strong!" in two days. That makes me happy, because I've always been athletic and strong, and I let some of that go these past ten years. It's time to reclaim my flexibility (both mental and physical), and my strength (bones, muscles, joints, ligaments, etc., even my skin!).

New sensations come, new concepts. Ideas. My field of vision widens, and I realize it's limitless. Time to follow my dreams to full vitality! I just hope I can continue each week without too much pain (if my former knee injuries caused by chondromalacia patella flare up). We'll see what next week brings. Saturday night is the hip-hop battle on campus. I'm looking forward to it!

CI. DANCE CLASS   MON. WED 10:30 - 12:20
2-11-20

Day 6

BIG DAY FOR FEELING - PAIN!

"LARGE AND SOFT" = JEAN'S WORDS.
I GOT INJURED. NOT MY PARTNER'S FAULT.
SHE WAS GENTLE AND SENSITIVE. I WAS FRAGILE

LEARNING TO ROLL & FLY WITH STOMACH OVER
BACK OF PARTNER.

MY PARTNER

OOPS!   ME →

HARD FLOOR

OUCH!

SHARP PAIN IN LEFT SHOULDER

2-13-20

Day 7

UNABLE TO DO FLOOR EXERCISES
WITH PARTNER. STILL IN PAIN +
HEALING PHASE. WATCHING, WRITING
AND DOING HAPPY DANCE IN SPHERICAL
SPACE (THE DANCE FLOOR). NEW
SENSATIONS + PARTICIPATORY EXPERIENCE
SHARING AT OPENING + CLOSING CIRCLE - ☺ —
SLOWLY OUTSIDE INNER SPACE IN ROOM

NOT SO BAD AT ALL SPACIOUSNESS

OK COOL!

ME WATCHING + DANCING

PEOPLE IN PAIRS ON GROUND

BREATHE   + WRITING IN JOURNAL ON BENCH

JEAN (GIVING GUIDANCE)
(VERY COOL)

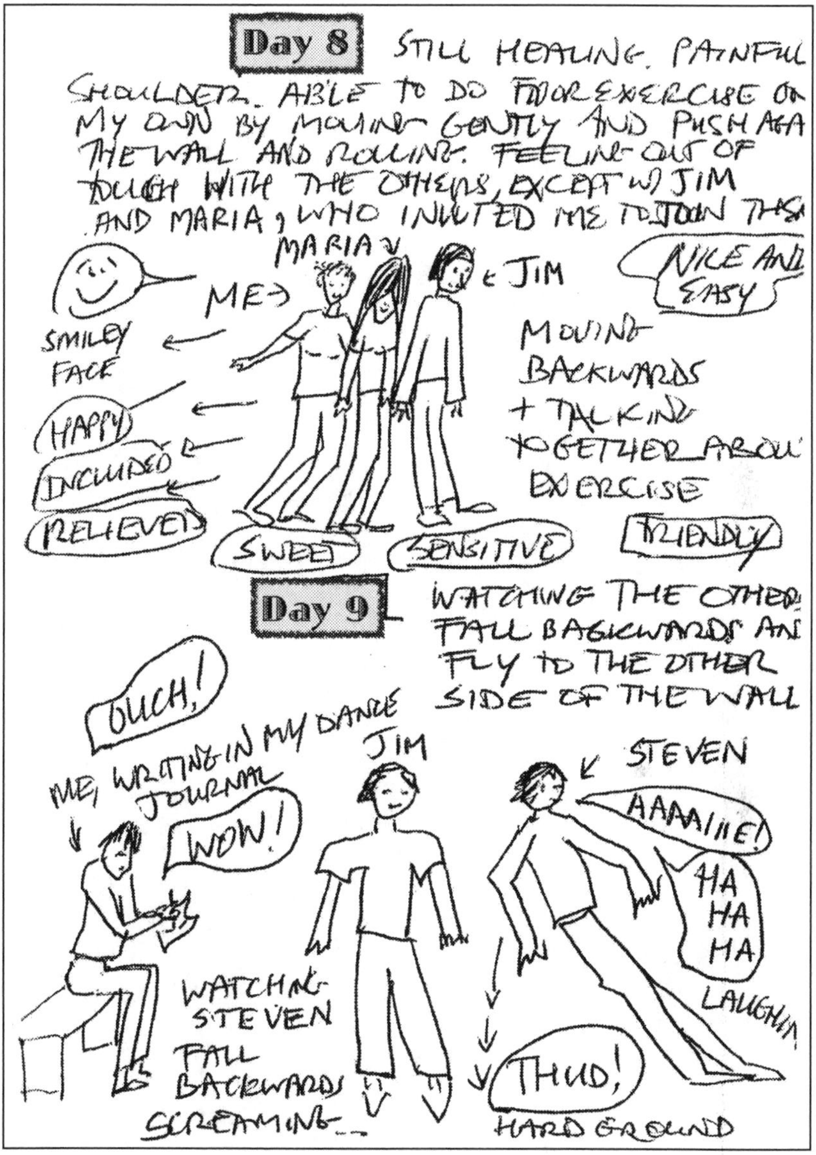

Sketchbook, Days 6 to 9

$\mathcal{F}$ebruary 10th, 2020, Monday, Day 6

We're at the end of class and I'm observing on the bench. I'm listening to Jean, who was explaining with Amy, my partner, because I got injured during an exercise with her. We were rolling over each other, and I didn't hurt my knee or neck, luckily, but my left shoulder was a bit hurt with carrying her weight. Jean asked if I wanted to go to ER and I said, "no." I'll put arnica on it and watch. She said to not immobilize it, to keep on moving it, so I massaged the arnica into my shoulder, and then I'm moving a bit—while writing and observing the others at the same time. It's not easy to multitask like this. I'm getting sweaty just watching them all roll all over each other in pairs.

If I were thirty or forty years younger, I bet I wouldn't have gotten injured like this. I think I pulled a shoulder muscle. I hope it will heal soon. She said to the class that we shouldn't feel pain, and if we do it means we're not using our skeletal support system like we should.

I see another student writing on the sidelines as well. I warmed up a lot this morning, doing the body scan to warm up my mind-body connection (thirty-five minutes), then stretching (fifteen minutes) at home, and ten more minutes at school. But I didn't expect to do such weight-bearing exercises in class, having a student—who is most likely much lighter than me—rolling over me or sitting on me. I tried to use my roundness and volume to support her, and vice versa, but it wasn't easy. I don't feel round on the floor, especially when rolling over someone else.

Jean just reminded us that our partner is a subject, not an object, and that this is high-risk activity, and that we have five fingers and five toes; we should strive to be softer and bigger in the point of contact. Jean sure has lots of good guidance and explanations about how to learn so much about our bodies and how they work together with gravity through space and on the floor.

February 11th, 2020, Tuesday

I'm sitting on my sofa with an ice pack. I took some ibuprofen (pain reliever) because my shoulder is really sore. It was so painful yesterday, I had to skip office hours to go get the ibuprofen pills and an ice pack after teaching for two hours. I know it was late—you're supposed to apply ice right away with injuries such as these—but I had all my students waiting for me (it took me longer to dress with one arm in pain) and student presentations. While I was teaching and trying not to lift or use my left arm, because I would get an acute shot of pain if I did, I was thinking that, "Yes, this is a high-risk activity," and that I was probably crazy to sign up for this course, even though it's super interesting, liberating, and empowering in so many ways. I'm fifty-five and most of the students are eighteen to twenty-two years old, I'd say, and their bodies aren't as fragile as mine. What was I thinking?

I remembered my aunt, who was a dancer, and now she's a psychologist. Right before the course started, we went out to dinner and she literally begged me not to take the course. She told me I'd get injured, and possibly disabled for life, if I took the course. I didn't want to believe her. She said, "I'm telling you this because I love you. PLEASE do not take that course." And I did, of course, despite what she said.

She had also told me not to move to a certain city in Europe to study, because she had and didn't like it when she was nineteen, like me, but I'd gone anyway and had a great experience. So, I figured this was the same thing. I'd get a completely different experience out of this dance course than what she had imagined, and I could laugh proudly and say to her in May, "You see, I took the whole course and never got hurt, except for a few bruises and sore knees at the beginning, and a few zits on my face from not being able to wash it after sweating for two hours, then teaching till 9:00pm on Mondays." But then I got hurt yesterday. And, unfortunately, it's pretty serious. Maybe she was right.

Last night, we did some gentle yoga at the mindfulness course that I'm helping teach. I'd still not been able to put ice on my shoulder, and it felt raw and ripped, despite the pain pills. I did as much as I could to participate. Luckily, I wasn't leading the gentle yoga this time, but it still hurt, so I backed off heavily. After class, a physical therapist put her arm on it and told me it might be my rotator cuff. She told me to ice it every hour for twenty minutes. Then she gave me a little bottle of aromatherapy for the pain. I'm not sure it will work, but at least it smells nice.

I thought back to what the neck doctors had said in Belgium ten years ago, and in the USA, about my neck and how fragile it was, and how I needed to avoid all contact sports, such as: soccer, martial arts, boxing, water skiing, skiing, jumping, etc., because of my precarious neck situation. And I realized how lucky I was that it was only my shoulder—and not the one I write with—that got injured. For once, my knees are fine, my neck is fine (it clicks a bit, but it's still attached to my head, thank goodness). So, this was a very close call.

Normally, I do yoga and swim on Tuesday mornings, but today, I'll go for a walk and work at home instead. I'll write Jean and tell her the truth: that I'm in pain and can't dance tomorrow with a partner (maybe alone), but I can't roll on the ground or move or lift my left arm. I'll ask her if I can just come to observe the class and participate in the opening and closing circles.

If I don't have to change clothes I can stay until twenty minutes after the hour, like the others. And I can take notes in my journal as I observe the class, the dancers, and Jean's instructions. It would be like dancing vicariously with the mind, instead of the body, tuning into my physical sensations and thoughts about dancing, while receiving Jean's guidance to the others, while watching them move on the floor. I did it for the last ten to fifteen minutes of class yesterday, while in pain, and surprisingly, I still got a lot out of it.

I don't want to abandon the class, but this physical setback—perhaps necessary to make me realize how high-risk an activity C.I. really is, like my aunt said, no, *screamed*, at me—is really eye opening and muscle jerking/tearing... maybe not tearing, but searing... These physical symptoms of pain and soreness kept me tossing to one side all night. It's funny, my partner hurt her back dancing with someone on Sunday, and she's five years younger than me. We both put arnica on ourselves last night and both suffered with pain. Is this our midlife crisis?

I hope Jean is understanding, and I hope she lets me observe the class and take notes, do the reading, attend the events, etc., without having to do things that could be potentially harmful to my body, from now on. It's sad, frustrating, and limiting; it reminds me of when I got injured on the track team as a sophomore in college and never ran again. That nearly broke me. I was depressed for six months and ended up leaving the country because of that injury.

This time, I'm wiser, and I have the tools of mindfulness, patience, and motivation to write books about this journey to keep me from dipping into the well of despair. And I have my partner, who fully supports me on this adventure, but she's now siding with my aunt and wants me to choose the bench instead of the 'battlefield.' These aren't her terms, they're mine.

If I were fifteen years old again, I'd be raring to go and ignore my pain. That's precisely what my dad taught me; it's what I did all of my youth, like running ten miles with an injured toe. Sure enough, I couldn't feel the pain anymore. I couldn't even feel the toe... for years afterwards. That's sort of what put him to his grave, I believe. Five hours of sports a day, and not listening to his body, ever, despite pain and agony. I don't want to end up like that. So, I'll listen to my body a lot, and back off, and make this a more virtual experience, while still embodying my feelings, asking my questions, and putting it all down in this journal.

What's weird is that the figures and words that I glued to decorate the cover of this journal are falling off now. They're coming unglued, like my body, in a certain sense. I'll glue them back on, with stronger, longer-lasting glue, and I'll do the same for my skeleton and muscles, by paying attention to my body as it heals. Pick up the pieces and learn from this experience. That's what I'm planning to do.

February 12th, 2020, Wednesday, Day 7

This is the first time I'm participating in class in a less physically participative way. Jean is allowing me to observe, write, and feel what is going on in the room, and to move around and do the happy dance—which is actually the small dance—and keep the room spherical.

I really enjoy exploring physical and mental sensations on my own—like a kid, when I would explore tiny wet blades of grass, their texture, smells, touch, etc.—while she explains what we are to do "as an invitation." And I can listen and choose to do the action, or movement, or pursue the intention. I can practice all the options, or not, by moving around the space on my own, being careful to not hurt my injured shoulder/arm, yet remain present and embody the movement with curiosity and awareness, just like I do, and teach, in my mindfulness practice and research.

This is dance research and it's powerful. It reminds me of an email I got yesterday from someone from CQ. They asked me to write an essay or article about my research and I wondered, "Is this the same CQ (Contact Quarterly) journal from our dance class? Or another publication?" I got excited about the idea of writing this kind of essay about dance research, and studying it from an academic, yet physical and cognitive perspective, through mindfulness awareness. We'll see. I'm still busy with all my other mindfulness research, and this physical/mental/social justice/inclusiveness dance research perspective makes my work all the more complete, and holistic.

Jean just told us that the last six inches towards the floor is where most people get injured. Then she looked at me with a smile. She's right. I'm not sure how exactly I got injured, but I'm sure it was within the last six inches towards the ground.

February 13th, 2020, Thursday

My shoulder still hurts, and I've iced it again. It's impossible to ice it while I'm at school or teaching, but I was able to ice it yesterday during lunch with the ice pack from my lunch box. I'll try that again tomorrow. Yesterday was great because I was able to stay for the closing circle. I usually have to change and run off to teach, but this time, I could hear the other students' impressions afterward and I could share my own. Most of them said things like they felt more connected to the others now, since they are dancing with them in very close quarters.

I saw them rolling on top of each other, like we did on Monday, which is how I got injured, yet they're doing it with mindful intention and awareness. Especially Greg, who has a broken foot. If I had that broken foot, I'd be more careful. I winced when I saw him walking around the room without his booty, and when he said it hurt after class. But he really wants to be a dancer, like most of them. Like I wanted to be when I was young, but couldn't, because of my bad knees. I'm so glad I'm taking this class despite my injury. It's giving me so much awareness about my own body and its self-imposed limitations.

Sure, I'm fifty-five, but I can still do a lot of things that many people my age can no longer do. In fact, last night, as I was getting ready for bed, I found myself walking—no, I was actually gliding—backwards towards the other side of our bathroom. It was only two or three steps, but I was swiftly moving backwards and had no fear. My balance was great, and I was thinking, "What the heck?" I was unable to do this before this dance class and we're only in the fourth week.

Also, yesterday, when I was making copies in the copy room at school, nobody was there, so I took advantage of the situation and did some interesting moves on the sleek floor. I kept my shoes on, but I soon realized how great they were for sliding, bending, and stretching. I had to be careful of my shoulder—always so careful now, it's such a pain—and I did a few light twirls, some lunges, a kick or two in the air, and nobody saw me—I think. And frankly, even if they did see me doing this, I'd just laugh and say, "Want to join me?" instead of making up an excuse.

This sort of reminds me of what my female protagonist in my first two novels does when she discovers the thrill of biking and swimming. She's only forty, though, but she goes wild in the bathroom at work with her newfound awareness of her body, and her muscles, which are growing stronger while shedding layers of fat and non-use. She's dancing and prancing around on the slippery floor in front of the mirror in a kind of bizarre ecstasy—through her discovery of self-empowerment and joy—when a colleague unexpectedly enters and makes fun of her.

How weird. I invented that scene about fifteen years ago when I wrote the manuscript for the book, when I was forty. And now, fifteen years later, I'm enacting it, but in the copy room at school, not the bathroom. And nobody came in to surprise me. Not yesterday. But I'll certainly do this again. I've taken over my body in so many ways. It's so liberating! And the social justice part is great, too. Jean and Susie and some of the other students, including Greg and Tina, went last night to the Black History Month event. I love how dance, justice work, research, and theory in all of these disciplines intertwine. It's so powerful for the students, and for me. What a way to make a huge difference in the world, one step, dip, jump, hop, and twirl at a time! ☺

February 14th, 2020, Friday

Below is my reaction to the hip-hop battle on campus that I submitted today to our course container. Here is my message to Jean with my submission: Please note, I submitted an image of my ticket as proof of attendance already and now I'm submitting my response. Sorry for going over the 500-word limit, I had lots to say, as usual!

I was very engaged by watching the hip-hop battle. I felt my arms and legs wanting to move, just like the dancers. I noticed that I held my breath a lot while they were moving, especially during the more acrobatic moves. My stomach was tight too, and towards the end, I got really hungry. I have a lot of empathy, so not only was I hungry, just watching them burn up calories, but my joints started to hurt from all of their moves on the floor.

I could smell some sort of dank sweat—I'm not sure if that's a term, but it wasn't like fresh sweat, it was like a rotten sweat, but it didn't bother me because I know how hard it is to dance like a maniac and try not to sweat. Impossible! I couldn't keep my eyes off the dancers, especially those who performed the best moves, in my opinion. Very original, daring, and dangerous.

I thought of the guy in the wheelchair near me. I hoped that he hadn't been injured dancing like this, and now he's confined to a wheelchair for life. I felt bad for him at first, and then I felt happy for him, because he came anyway to support his friends and that was beautiful to see. I sensed gravity pulling me down in my chair, and also lifting me up. I wanted to get up and dance with them several times, but I couldn't. I had a nagging feeling: "Who am I to think that I can dance like that?" since I've never taken a hip-hop class. Then another nagging feeling kept telling me to get my butt off the chair and make myself turn into a dancer, and a fool, in front of everyone.

Of course, I listened to my first nagging voice and sat there with my butt glued to the chair, and my hands grasping its sides to keep my body from springing up. My reflexes are really fast, probably from all that martial arts and tennis training, so I felt twitches inside my stomach muscles and chest muscles when I watched the dancers. I also felt the twitches when the young woman next to me kept yelling, "Yes!" I wanted to yell just like her, but I was shy.

It's interesting to think about how my identity informs how I see things. I'm much older than everyone on the dance floor, and most of the audience as well. I saw the dancers as if I were one of them, however. I've always been like this. It's genetic, because my mom and my grandma also had this quality. We could mingle with people four times younger than us and not feel a difference, as if we were the same exact age. My grandma passed away, but my mom and I can both be with younger folks and relate as if we were one of them. I think it's a quality, or perhaps a talent, but I don't do anything to be like this. I was born this way. The hard part is looking in the mirror afterwards and realizing I've packed away many more years than the people I was just mingling with.

During the battle, I really thought I could be one of them with lots of practice (and knee pads). My physical state made a difference when watching and responding to this event. I was tired because I'd just done an author panel and book presentation and signing for about thirty women, mainly from India. I'd had to come out as a lesbian author to them and I didn't know how accepting they'd be of me. It went well, and I sold quite a few books, but it was quite stressful. So, I was tired and hungry when I came to watch the battle this evening, but as it went on, I found myself smiling the entire time, very enthusiastic, and cheering for many of the dancers.

In fact, I can totally relate what I saw within this hip-hop battle to our Contact Improvisation research. There were so many elements that demonstrated a thorough knowledge of gravity, special awareness, sensitivity and consent to one's dance partner/battle partner, etc. Flexibility, mindfulness (although it went much faster than what we're doing so far in class), alertness… it seems very similar, but there's much more rapid action and even a bit of aggressiveness (probably faux aggressiveness, because they all seemed to care about each other, even in direct competition).

Certain divergent aspects were the expressive facial and finger/ hand gestures in hip hop, which I haven't seen in our C.I. class yet. Sticking out tongues, the middle finger, etc., or flipping sneakers or hats in the air. Maybe these will come with time, we're only in our fourth week of class.

A lot of hip hop seems political to me: the music, the words in the music, gestures, attitudes, and strength. Given the article that we read about the history of hip hop, this makes complete sense. The identities of the dancers seem to inform their movement in various ways, such as being masculine (some of the dancers whom I believed to identify as women—they seemed feminine in appearance—had very masculine gestures and movements, for example).

Some of the incredibly flexible dancers whom I believed to identify as men—they looked like men to me because they seemed masculine in appearance—were very skinny, yet strong and extremely flexible with their arm and leg muscles. They made fluid dance movements that made them look like wound-up ballerinas going at two-hundred miles per hour, so that gave them a more feminine appearance.

In addition to gender identity and expression, there seemed to be a mixture of races, ethnicities, and ages. Most seemed able-bodied to me, because they were doing so many difficult moves.

Lastly, your question about connecting the practice of radical independence and responsible citizenship within this event would take me four pages at least to answer, so I'll leave this one alone. If you really want me to attempt to answer it, I can do so in a future missive.

Jean's response surprised me: "I am genuinely obsessed with radical independence and responsible citizenship, so if you ever decide to write 4 pages on it, feel free to email it me." Well, I'll certainly let her know when I've written those four pages!

Next, I created a list of questions about the hip-hop battle. I'm not sure who I can ask these questions, but we needed to submit a list. It was actually fun coming up with these:

1) Which kinds of moves in hip hop do you prefer and why?
2) What's your favorite music to dance hip hop? Why?

3) Describe your most dangerous time dancing hip hop, where was it, who were you with, and what went through your head as it was happening to you, or to your partner?

4) What is the potential value of teaching hip hop, and how to conduct hip-hop battles, to kids in school from a social justice perspective?

5) What would you do if you could never dance hip hop again? Or is this a question that you'd never even consider answering?

6) What did your parents/guardians/teachers say when they first saw you dancing hip hop? How did you deal with their reaction?

7) How do you feel gravity when you dance hip hop? How does it inform your movements and speed?

8) How does the music affect your moves when you dance hip hop?

9) Is there any kind of hip-hop music that you can't stand? Why?

10) What is it like dancing hip hop in front of spectators? Do you like it when they cheer you or your battle partner on?

11) Do you ever wake up at night and want to start dancing right there next to your bed? Do you ever do it, even if it's 2am? Why or why not?

12) What other activity/sport would you practice if you had to give up hip hop one day? Why?

February 16th, 2020, Sunday

I went to our Sunday 5Rhythms dance session today even though my shoulder has not yet healed. I've been taking ibuprofen and arnica pills, and putting a mixture of arnica cream/gel and Chinese and Japanese liquid pain-relief medications on it, and trying not to use it too much by not carrying heavy objects, etc. It reminds me of when I hurt my shoulder in volleyball (the other shoulder), and I couldn't swim or do sports for over a year because it turned into tendonitis. It happened again about ten years later, and it was really painful, since it became a serious shoulder (rotator cuff) injury. I hope that won't happen this time. I really want to heal because I want to dance fully without pain, and continue to do yoga and swim, and even be able to put on my shirts and sweaters again.

Today's 5Rhythms class was different because normally I dance all over the place in a wild and energetic way, especially when it's *Staccato* or *Chaos* (the second and third of the five rhythms). Today, however, because I didn't want to hurt my shoulder any more than necessary, I danced more on the fringes of the group. There were about twenty-five of us at the studio where we dance every Sunday.

I tried to stay away from weaving in and out of the group because of my injury. But in the end, Maya, our teacher/facilitator, put on some really cool music for *Lyrical*, and then for *Flowing*, the fourth and first rhythms, and I couldn't stop myself. I danced almost like usual, weaving in and out, moving forwards and backwards, up and down, spinning, twisting, but not jumping, pulling, or rolling on the floor. I usually do that too.

I found myself feeling very sad, and even depressed, during *Chaos* at first. Maybe it was because she'd bought a new speaker, so with three huge speakers in the room the music seemed really loud and violent. I wanted more relaxing and soothing music, at a volume much softer. I always want to turn down the volume because I have really sensitive ears. So, I was sad as I stood on one leg, clinging to a dance bar. It was one of those wooden bars for ballet dancers, by a big window, overlooking the restaurant next door. To tell the truth, I wanted to be anywhere but there.

Then the music got better, and softer, and I was able to fly again. I felt my face light up; my smile wouldn't stop, and I literally felt like I was floating amongst everyone on the dance floor. It was like spreading melted butter on toast with my feet—so smooth, airy, and effortless. I didn't lose my breath, but I knew it was a workout because I was bending all parts of my body at once, especially my knees, ankles, and spine, and I was racing at a fast pace all over the room. It was exhilarating!

That happened twice, with two songs that I particularly liked: one by Snatam Kaur, and the other one, Lady Marmalade (*Voulez-vous coucher avec moi ce soir?*). That was the song that my first dance teacher, Pepper, introduced to us when I was in the seventh grade or so. She was amazing; I really looked up to her during that summer dance course. So, when the song came on, I danced like I did as a kid—energetic (without hurting my shoulder as best as I could) and moving around again with that silly smile stuck on my face.

Now, I'm home, icing my shoulder, sipping tea, and wondering if we'll have more dance articles to read for tomorrow's class. Last Sunday night I read all three. It was a lot to take in, but they were superb articles and I looked forward to discussing them in Jean's class. Our hip-hop battle reflection is due tomorrow morning, and I submitted mine on Friday, so maybe she'll give us less homework this week. It's fun being a student again, but it does take up some time—lots of time, actually. I'm glad I'm only teaching three classes this semester and the mindfulness course. Otherwise, it would be too much.

February 17th, 2020, Monday, Day 8

I'm watching Jean demonstrate some moves in front of the class with two students. She's pushing on their butt bones—they are upside-down—and it's interesting, watching her give us 'survival training,' so that if and when we fall, we won't get hurt. It requires figuring out our body's organization. I can't do it because my shoulder hurts, and she's okay with me doing what I can alone, and then slowly dancing 'on the fringes,' so that I can be part of this class, but still experience what she's teaching from a peripheral perspective. This exercise, pushing on the back of one's partner's pelvis, would be really hard on my wrists, hands, knees, and pelvis. I'm more comfortable watching, taking in her words, and watching the others do it. Of course, I learn more when I practice all the exercises, but since I can't (or shouldn't) do it physically, right now, I'm comfortable with this different way of learning.

Today, when I came in, there was some neat music playing on the stereo, and because it was a bit loud, I put in my special ear plugs. Thirty years ago, I wouldn't have done that, but as I age, I've become increasingly sensitive to noise, touch, smells, and sounds, so I need devices like these to protect me.

We did an exercise where we put our stomachs on the floor and really felt the ground through mindfulness, by paying attention to our bellies. She called it "belly… something," and then we moved our limbs really slowly. I felt fortunate to be able to do this exercise with the others. Now, my shoulder hurts again, so I'm going to take my arnica pills, and then ibuprofen, towards the end of class, and put some arnica cream on my shoulder again. It even hurts when I write in this journal. I'm feeling hot just writing right now, so I'll do that and then move around the room again. It's fun to prance around and watch the others, while staying centered to my own experience.

I've discovered that I like doing the exercises against the wall instead of the floor. There's less gravity, so it hurts less. They're now doing some exciting pair work to understand how to ride the wave of the rhythm of your partner's pelvis. "It's exhausting," Jean said, "... and how do we work with that? Organizing the mass of our bodies with physics." I'm concerned because Greg is doing this exercise with a partner, with his booty and broken foot, and he was twirling and fell, and got up again. That made me feel badly for him. He's continuing to move really fast around the room, despite this fall, which made a big "clunk." I wonder if anyone else feels his potential pain and/or self-inflicted damage like me?

It's nice to finally know the names of everyone, except for the new young woman who started with us today. I'm going to continue to move around the room, and pretend to track my partner's rhythm, even though I don't have a partner. It's not about mimicking the partner's moves; it's about "riding the edges of their bones," and navigating the relationship between feet and pelvis, learning to orient ourselves in space: weight shifting and sensing the mass; not creating it but riding it like a wave in the ocean. Jean said, "Inviting your partner into your body, leaning in with hips and ribs, etc., putting weight on outer feet, having arms up, leaning away."

It is nice because Marie and Jim asked me to join them as they walked backwards while talking about what it was like to do this exercise. Jim said he was exhausted. They asked me what it was like for me, too, as I watched. That was super nice and inclusive of them!

February 19th, 2020, Wednesday, Day 9

I'm watching everyone practice their survival skills by running across the room. They're folding and sailing into the wall, three or four at a time, falling into space, running, spiraling, twisting, spinning, watching the weight of their pelvis, streaming, researching without the head—with the body—taking the slack out of their bodies, being able to catch the wind with every part of their physical entities, like a sail. Jean is demonstrating with Susie how you can fall and coordinate the sphericity of your body.

It's interesting, Jean often says "their" instead of "hers" or "his." She's super inclusive when it comes to pronouns. She's called me "they" as well, and I haven't corrected her. I'm trying to open my mind about these things. It's true that I've always been androgynous, so I guess it's normal that she wouldn't simply assume that I'm a "she."

When Susie fell backwards, Jean let go. I got nervous. She fell like at Six Flags on a ride, but she was flexible and didn't fall to the ground and hurt herself. It was fascinating to see how Susie recovered and flew to the other side of the room, like a bird spinning on her toes, arms flailing, and very light. It was amazing to watch.

Steven and Jim are right in front of me and laughing like crazy because Steven fell backwards on his butt on the hard floor. He screamed as he was falling and landed with a huge "thud!" Everyone laughed a bit, and Jean asked if Steven was okay. I also asked him, and he insisted he wanted to try it again, saying: "It's very scary. Your feet want to go out." When he was explaining what it felt like to do this, he said he only saw his own shadow on the floor, so it was quite scary. Now, he's laughing nervously as he spins and runs backwards towards the other side of the room. I can't do this because it's a high-risk activity, like almost everything we do in this class. Jean repeats that fact a lot.

But I did participate in the small dance as we danced around the room with ourselves—with our eyes slightly open to *feel* the room and the dancers. We were trying to see what it felt like to be round and spherical and know and feel the difference. When Jim asked what the difference was, Jean said she wasn't the expert, so we were all going to try to figure it out. That's such a distinctive way of teaching—so student-focused and experiential.

It's really interesting to watch how people fall. It's funny, the guys—there are only three—scream more than the girls, but one guy, Greg, is finally sitting out and writing in his journal while lying on his back on the ground. I felt bad for him as he flew through the air on his broken foot. He twisted and jumped even. Unlike him, I was afraid of colliding with the other dancers and getting hurt.

I still feel pain in my shoulder, but I did do a bit of gentle yoga yesterday at home. It helped with my mobility, and removed some of the constant, dull pain. How are we supposed to be "soft in the front of the ankles?" as Jean instructs us? By falling backwards, trusting the other person to support your weight, catching you as you fall, keeping the roundness, the soft knees, and soft feet. Both partners are supposed to do this.

Unfortunately, while they were practicing, Stacy fell and got hurt. I waited a while because Susie, her partner, was sitting with her. I just asked and Stacy says she's okay and thanked me for asking. I'm watching what everyone is doing. It's the same exercise that I did with my partner—and it's how I got hurt—a week ago.

Jean just demonstrated with Belinda how to roll and stay suspended in the air, over your partner's pelvis, and feel your toes using proprioception. It was really cool. Belinda was suspended like an airplane, and Jean was on her hands and knees. Belinda needed to feel the floor through Jean's shoulders and knees/pelvis. The under-person needs to do the small dance and have a soft belly orientation (not position), and the over-person also needs a soft belly. They either go across the pelvis or diagonally across the shoulders and pelvis, I think.

Now I know how I got injured. I was underneath, and not doing the small dance, and my partner was suspended and rolling over my spine, in the middle of my back, instead of my pelvis, and I couldn't support her weight with my shoulder. At least, now, I know!

Day 10

ROLLING ON THE FLOOR ALONE WHILE EVERYONE ROLLS TOGETHER ACROSS THE ROOM. FEELING ALONE YET CONNECTED.

WHAT ARE THEY THINKING OF ME? I DON'T CARE. PROTECTING MY BODY. BODY-MIND CONNECTION. FEELING MY ROUNDNESS ON THE HARD FLOOR. RELAX - ESCAPE - FREEDOM.

WALL

EVERYONE ROLLING TOGETHER

ME, ALONE, IN SMALL CIRCLES
ROLLING VERY SLOWLY
STILL PAINFUL CONSCIOUSLY
✓ BEING CAREFUL TIME FLIES!

NO JUDGING, ONLY SELF-JUDGEMENT

JEAN SAYS IT'S OK TO STAY

Day 11

REALLY INCLUSIVE!

Mindfulness

SITTING IN A SHARING CIRCLE FOR HALF THE CLASS. start 3/1 3/3!
I'VE GOT A SMILE PASTED ON MY FACE. HAPPY TO LISTEN AND SHARE.

LAUGHTER   QUESTIONS

DEEP THOUGHT

STRENGTH

NO ATTITUDE!

JEAN
LYING DOWN IS STILL OK!

LIGHTNESS + SPACIOUSNESS RESPECT + INQUIRY

ME

REALLY NICE CIRCLE

ALL THE STUDENTS I KNOW MOST OF THEIR NAMES... REALLY NICE!!

SUSIE

WE MOVE AND STRETCH AND BOUNCE AS WE LISTEN AND SHARE. SO COOL!

Day 12

SENSATIONS
A BIT OF FEAR
BUT ALSO LIGHTNESS
OF BEING
SOFTNESS, FIRMNESS
SHIFTING POSITIONS
BLENDING INTO THE MOVE-MENT

NEW EXERCISE
WORKING WITH ANOTHER
+ GRAVITY — LIGHTLY,
PURPOSELY, NOT EASY
FEELING + SENSING
GRAVITY + THE FLOOR
ROLLING ON
FLOOR W/
PARTNER

INTERESTING

SLOWLY
TRYING TO
FEEL +
NOT BE
SELF-CONSCIOUS

FEELING THE OTHER'S
MOVEMENTS + BREATH
TURNING, SLOWLY UNWINDING

SHARING
SPACE

Day 13

PROBABLY BECAUSE

ONE STUDENT
SAID TO ME,
"YOU'RE SO CUTE!"

I'M SO
OLD

I'D LIKE TO
JOIN THEM BUT
I SHOULDN'T

ME TWISTING +
TURNING —
FEELING LIGHT
ON MY FEET
IN A CORNER

SMILING

ME

A
STUDENT

WRITING IN
MY JOURNAL
FURIOUSLY
AS EVERYONE
DANCES.
WATCH HIM
+ LISTEN IN

THIS IS SO COOL!

A BREAK FROM
REALITY

SELF-CONSCIOUS

ROLLING AGAINST
EACH OTHER PLAYFULLY

Sketchbook, Days 10 to 13

$\mathcal{F}$ebruary 24th, 2020, Monday, Day 10

I'm in class again after a weekend where I spent all Sunday on the computer, unfortunately. I felt it in my injured shoulder. Then I took out the trash without thinking and felt a sharp pain again. So, I'm being careful again today in class. My acupuncturist gave me an ointment from China that I'm putting on twice a day, and that's helping with the pain. Jean had us roll on the floor across the room for about ten minutes and I quickly realized that it was best for me to roll back and forth in a corner, slowly, at my own pace, instead of rolling like the others. This was softer, and I could be more careful and respectful of my injured shoulder.

Jean's now having everyone work in pairs to see how to move with the stomach, pelvis, and shoulders without strain. They're stretching and being very soft and fluffy, in a way, with a twist. Like a dishrag. She demonstrated with Susie because nobody else volunteered. I didn't want to get hurt, so I'm going to try it on my own in the corner. She says that there's a moment of counterbalance that helps with organization. There sure is a lot of unexpected organization in contact improvisation. I never would've guessed.

Today, I offered to take four people in my car downtown from 7:00 to 10:00pm on a Monday evening, once I'm done volunteering with the mindfulness class. Next week is my last week, so I'll be happy to drive the students after that. Susie also volunteered, and it would be fun if we all went together as a class. I don't think I could do all the contact improv stuff, but I could participate in the one-hour class, and then watch the others practice, like I'm doing now. Apparently, it's in a back alley, so I'll be glad to go with others, and not alone.

Also, I sent Jean an email on Wednesday afternoon to see if I could still continue to do what I'm doing in class. I'm not exactly the most active participant. But I do really care about the class and learning as much as I can with the others, even though I'm so limited due to my injury. I didn't hear back, so I figured either she's super busy, or she doesn't want me to continue. I figured it was the former option, so I came today. I didn't get a chance to read my emails this morning, and when I came to class, she said she'd responded this morning and yes, I could continue as long as I felt like I was getting something out of the class—which I am.

That's a relief.

So, now I'm watching her, and Susie, demonstrate the surfing and rolling exercise on the floor, like I did when I got injured two weeks ago. It's a low-level point of contact while they're rolling on the floor, a bigger and softer point of contact. I'm going to try it alone now. Jean just showed us, with Susie, how to move above and below each other by dispersing and reversing their weight to find the clearest pathway. I tried it on my own, watching the others in pairs, rolling smoothly over each other, like taquitos, and then I did my own rolling on the floor at the edge of the room. As I was doing it, I felt a huge release of muscle tension; but in my left shoulder and arm, I felt more pain, despite the release elsewhere, as I rolled over the floor, slowly twisting and turning on my back, sides, face, front, etc., at my own spiraling pace.

I just put arnica on my shoulder, which felt good. It's already 11:55am—amazing! Nearly the whole class period is over; it's gone really fast. It's neat to see how Jean and Susie are having fun, and Susie is actually Jean's boss, and friend. I can't imagine doing this kind of horizontal dance, bodies intertwined, with any of my bosses—ever. At a certain point, Jean was underneath, and Susie was above her, lying on her back. Then Jean stood up, and Susie did, too. They moved like one person at the same time.

It was really cool, and I wanted to clap at the show, but we all snapped our fingers instead. That's what we always do here. I'm not sure why, but it's probably so we don't disturb the other classes, or else it's to contain our energy, so we can use it on the dance floor. I'm going to do the happy dance and walk/prance slowly around the room as I observe the others in pairs. They seem to be having fun. They're all smiling at least!

February 26th, 2020, Wednesday, Day 11

Today was interesting because we started class ten minutes late. Most of the students, except for Susie, Jean and me, were sitting on the ground, next to the bench, talking in a small circle. They knew it was time to start class, but they stayed there, far away. I wondered if they thought we were having a private faculty talk or something and they were just being polite.

Finally, Jean said, "How interesting." Then, after a while, they joined us. No sudden movements, no shame, threats, or humiliation. She just called it "interesting" and "different than usual," and we went on with the class. She's really got a different style of teaching, how she addresses the students, with so much respect, warm-heartedness, and curiosity. I've taught for twelve years, and I'm surprised at how much I'm learning from her.

We spent an hour talking in a large circle. It was cool because before, I'd have been really angry and thinking to myself, 'Isn't this a dance class? Aren't we supposed to be moving/dancing?' And I would've gotten frustrated at the slow pace of things. But I didn't. I really enjoyed the slow pace at the beginning of class that spread into more than an hour. I look forward to dance class to start off my teaching day because it's slow, yet it's really deep and profound. We may not move a lot; that is, I may not move a lot, unlike the others, but it has a huge effect on my day. I dive into depths that I don't usually reach, especially at school.

We sat in a circle on the hard floor and I realized that these past six weeks, sitting on the hard floor twice a week for two hours, and rolling around on it, too, has taught me not to hurt while sitting with my legs crossed or outstretched. Sure, I still shift a bit, and Jean encourages us to keep moving as we sit, which is so cool, because we can't do that anywhere else in society except for in dance classes, gymnastics classes, and nursery schools, I imagine.

So, I shift, stretch, pull, and lie down, and nobody cares—they're doing the same, and Jean and Susie are, too. It's so relaxing and inclusive, this space. We can say what we really think, and we all have an equal shot at it. We passed the pen in our opening circle today. The other day it was a stick of lip balm. The person who has the pen, or lip balm, is the one who can talk. The others simply listen, and ask questions afterwards, if they want to. I found myself smiling because I felt safe, curious, accepted, energized, and especially connected to everyone, even though I'm a faculty member and old enough to be their parent, or even grandparent!

We're learning a ton about each other as a group—and being vulnerable. We're sharing things about our thoughts, bodies, experiences, and emotions that I certainly didn't think we'd share in this class. It's so different from any other class I've ever taken—or taught. I'm really impressed with everyone. It's humbling, as Jean told me when I wrote her and praised her teaching style.

After all the sharing, which had us laughing a bit, I spoke about the times I laid down in the faculty room wearing a suit, hoping nobody would see me in the corner. I mentioned how one time, a female colleague I didn't know came in to put her lunch in the fridge, and I popped up into a half-lotus position, pretending to meditate. Then I showed what I'd done to the group; I didn't describe it. People laughed at that. I'd figured that meditating, sitting in half-lotus, was less weird than lying in *Savasana* on the cold floor in a corner and doing the happy dance in my head. I was right. The colleague smiled and went on her way.

After we had all shared, we moved. We did little rolls and crescents (like croissants), and helixes, amongst other things, and then we paired up with someone. I asked Tina if she'd work with me, without touching. She agreed. She'd shared that she didn't really want to be touched today, or at least she requested that we clearly ask her, before touching. So, I decided that she'd be a good partner for the exercise because I didn't want to be touched either, with my sore shoulder, which was healing, but still... and she was sitting right next to me.

We watched each other do the exercise, then shared our

impressions, then we listened to each other's thoughts about what we did as we moved, and it was really cool. I said that I felt self-conscious because my T-shirts—I had on two, one layered over the other—didn't cover my belly as I rolled over, and since my belly was round and soft, I was embarrassed.

She said, "So you're feeling self-conscious about your clothes coming up," and I said, "Yeah," and I repeated the part about my belly.

I've always been self-conscious about it, and I've always had a belly, even as a kid, even when I looked like a beanstalk to the outer world. I had this belly under my T-shirt for nobody to see. I hid it. But when I played tennis in high school, and I was so short, they called me "brine shrimp," and then "hangover," because my tummy hung over my shorts. Then I grew too fast—fourteen inches in a year, I think—and got scoliosis, and I had to become a swimmer to fix it.

Anyway, the class was great today; time flew, and I didn't even sit on the sidelines, or write. I did it all slowly, and painfully, but I did it! I'm looking forward to going downtown soon on a Monday night to take Jean's C.I. class, and eat tacos afterwards. I'm pretty sure I know where she goes. I love those tacos!

March 2nd, 2020, Monday, Day 12

I unfortunately fell going upstairs last night. I was carrying things in both hands, and I'd shut off the hall light. I don't know why I did that, but it wasn't a smooth move. I was in my head, my mind was working on my teaching files, due Wednesday, and I was tired from a weekend non-stop conference in Southern California and then driving all the way home. So, I stumbled, falling upwards, then down. I'm pretty sure my spine got compressed, especially on the right side, in the middle, and my left hip/thigh muscle hurt too, and, of course, my left shoulder, which was already hurting from the stress of the conference. I was exhausted after not sleeping well at the hotel, eating too much at the buffet meals, lack of yoga and walking, and being indoors in air conditioning and fluorescent lights for two days.

It's not an excuse, but it's a testimony to my lack of balance when I don't spend enough quality time in my body, when I stay stuck in my mind, and it shows my propensity to being a klutz, as I've always been a bit distracted when I move: stubbing toes, slamming fingers in doors, falling up and down stairs, clipping corners, etc.

Today, I mentioned this in class, briefly. Jean congratulated me on using the term 'falling up,' as opposed to stumbling, or falling down. Then we did an exercise where we worked in partners—and I thought, since I'd created my new injuries, which I treated with arnica gel and arnica pills—that I wouldn't work with a partner, but I was wrong. Jean rolled over on the floor towards me and we did the exercise together, even though I was somewhat in pain. It was interesting, challenging, and a bit scary to do this exercise with her, since she's the teacher and has so much experience. And I'm such a novice, I felt really aware of my jumpy nerves.

In fact, I asked a dumb question about the skeleton she brought to class this morning. Adults have 206 bones, and babies have about seventy more, apparently, and I told her I hadn't read the two articles that were due, and I felt really bad about that, but I just couldn't with my teaching file to complete, so much work to do, and the conference. One of the articles was about the skeletal system, and I felt dumb asking this question, "Do babies have more bones than adults for protection?" But I asked it anyway.

Jean responded that babies' bones are fused together as we get older, like in the skull at the top, for protection as adults. I felt stupid, and as soon as I said it, I realized that everyone had probably figured out that I didn't read the article. Once again, I felt like a student who hadn't done her homework, like a naughty kid. At least I was learning what it was like to be a student again, with all its positive and negative sides to it. That will probably help me relate to my students better.

When we did the rolling and touching on the floor, and Jean asked what the sensations were like, I felt self-conscious. She said to pay attention to the point of contact, and movement, roundness, and touch, to feel where our partner is moving, and going to move, to anticipate it, and see what that feels like. I know that it'd be easier if I hadn't been self-conscious in my head. I usually don't touch people with my body—unless it's my partner, or when I'm giving a hug to a close friend or family member—so it's strange for me, and I know I'm in my head, and worrying about what I feel like (chubby tummy), what I might smell like (freshly washed clothes, but maybe the detergent is too strong smelling?), a bit sweaty in my fleece sweater, my socks, etc. Now I have to leave early to go to a meeting, exceptionally, and I forgot to tell Jean. Ooops! Anyway, I'm learning a lot, even though I can't do all the exercises. At least I'm trying!

March 4th, 2020, Wednesday, Day 13

I'm able to do some of the partner exercises again today. It's really nice to feel a part of the group again. We started with movement, instead of sitting in the circle. "The idea invites us into reality. Breathing is a resource. The point of contact can stay soft, and big, and then it's available to roll." These were some of Jean's instructions today, as we worked in pairs, putting our bodies in the form of a crescent (like a croissant, while leaning into each other's side, and moving around in circles). "Your spine doesn't have to collapse," she reminded us.

I did a few movements alone, dancing, and prancing around the room to warm up, and twirling, etc. And then I worked with about four partners, including Susie and Jean, or maybe five, and it was fun to pair up with them. It was interesting to see some of them smile after we worked together. It was tricky, because they couldn't see me, or my head, and I couldn't see theirs because we had our butts together.

Jean also said, "It appears that the feet are round, instead of flat." Apparently, a lot of this has to do with the mind, the imagination, feeling space, and awareness. "The legs should always be a little bit bouncy, like a trampoline," she added. One student didn't go all the way to the end of the room, and Jean said, "Let's go the whole way together." And they each catapulted their way across the room. Then she said, "The lungs inflate the capacity of the body."

When I'm writing Jean's words, I'm not sure if I'm getting them right, but the main idea is there: "Inflate the balloon into the point of contact. Once you find the connection, if you move the feet, sometimes, it gets easier."

I saw Jean talking to a police officer who had been standing outside, watching us. I wondered what that was about. Then we got another demonstration from Jean and two students, and it was really cool. "It's not a position you're orienting... There's the yummy spot..." She explained how our attention goes into the body, but we need to focus on *all* the body, and our partner's feet, and the point of contact with the floor (in this case, it was knees, hands and arms). Really smooth, really cool stuff.

Then Jim asked, "Limbs are allowed?"

Jean nodded, "Yes, limbs are allowed."

As I sit here on the bench, I find my thoughts wandering back to the conversation I had for nearly an hour with my Department Chair about classes, and my frustrations, right before coming to dance class this morning. What a breath of fresh air (it's a cliché, but it's true), to come here, move around the room (wildly), be taught, learn, interact with the others (and myself), and get out of my head! What an intense relief. And I don't want the class to end today. It's so wonderful to think, and do, something so different from my usual life!!! What a gift.

SPECIAL DAY BUT **Sunday** 5 Rhythms

(∵ PARTNER SICK)

LOUD MUSIC   LIGHTNESS   FRENCH SONGS

= EARPLUGS   JOY/EXTASY   LOUD MUSIC

ME   LYRICAL

←SWEATING   WORRYING ABOUT CORONAVIRUS

JERKING   (NO HUGS, NO

STACCATO   KISSES, NO TOUCHING

STILLNESS   TWIRLING   HAND SANITIZER,

PEACE   SPINNING   WINDOWS OPEN

DEFYING   WIPING DOWN FLOORS

GRAVITY   AND HANDLES, ETC —

Day 14   PARTICIPATING FULLY

WITH PARTNERS (S)

MOVING TWISTING SLOWLY,

TURNING, SENSING, DOING HAPPY DANCE

COOL   W/ PARTNER'S HAPPY DANCE

DOWN TO THEIR FEET.

TAKING TIME TO BREATHE

AND SENSE THEIR ENERGY

AND MOVEMENT

EYES SLIGHTLY CLOSED.

→ SOFT, SMOOTH, SELF-

CONSCIOUS

TALKING LATER IN WHISPERS)

—DEBRIEF (SORRY I

HAPPY DANCE   TOUCHED YOUR BLACK HAIR

SHARING W/ PARTNER AT HOME   W/O ASKING) —ITS OK!

TAKING THIS VIRUS SERIOUSLY. 100% SHIFT FROM 2 DAYS AGO

Day 15

O/ SCARED

OUR LAST CLASS AT SCHOOL

CORONAVIRUS IS TAKEN SERIOUSLY — ALL CLASSES ONLINE MAYBE? IMPOSSIBLE

16 PEOPLE CAME — LAST CLASS

PRACTICING SOCIAL DISTANCING TO STAY SAFE

STAYING 6 FEET APART. WORKING ALONE, BREATHING, SENSING, MOVING, PELVIS ON FLOOR

ME TOO!

& ME — THIS IS SAD. — WHATS NEXT?

I LIVE ALONE, WHAT WILL I DO?

WORRIES

GIVING US HER NUMBER "I'LL BE YOUR ROCK"

WHERE WILL I LIVE? IN DORMS

JEAN REASSURING. JUMPING UP — NO WORDS. PHYSICAL RESPONSE.

Day 16

WEEK 10 (2 — WEEK BREAK)

DOING HAPPY DANCE ALONE IN MY LIVING ROOM (FACING MY PATIO OT THE SCREEN)

WEIRD AT HOME

DON'T LOOK AT SCREEN

SELF-CONSCIOUS

COMPUTER SCREEN (EVERYONE ON IT W/ ZOOM — JEAN'S GUIDING (15 PARTICIPANTS)

EYES CLOSED

RELIEF! ALL TOGETHER!

BALANCING

ROUND NESS OF BODY

ALONE

WOBBLY

TABLE + COMPUTER

HEARING TODDLER SOUNDS + BIRDS (CHIRPING) A BIT ANNOYING) TUNING IT OUT + BEING WHOLE

EARTH'S ENERGY

← RIDING THE WAVES OF THE EARTH. FEELING ROUND FEET + BODY + SURFING

Sketchbook, Sunday & Days 14 to 16

March 8th, 2020, Sunday, 5Rhythms

I decided to include my experience dancing at 5Rhythms in my journal today because it's also a dance form and it's greatly influenced how I interpret dance, and life. Like this course on campus, it's made a huge difference in my perception of the world. I got there really early because I had to drop friends off at the airport first. It took a while to warm up to soothing, slow, flowing music. Then I limbered up my body by flowing around the room, forwards, backwards, and sideways, with big, round movements, with my arms, hands, and hips. Well, I tried that, but my hips aren't that flexible, unfortunately. Twenty-four years after taking belly-dance lessons for six months in Brussels, in 1996, my swivel hips are more like fused hips.

When I watched our 5Rhythms teacher, Maya, I saw that I had a long way to go to loosen this part of my body again. I felt rusty there, or perhaps just not that feminine. I'm working on it though.

It was weird because, usually, we all hug and touch a bit before, during, and after our dance sessions, but everyone's now careful about not catching the coronavirus (COVID-19), so we're trying to wash our hands a lot, and use sanitizer, wipes, etc., to keep clean. I did end up rolling on the floor some, and I know our teacher had it vacuumed, because I saw one of the participants doing it when I walked in.

Maya showed us afterwards how to decline—with a hand in front of us to say "no" without speaking—if someone dances in our space, to let them know we don't want this. I was the volunteer she chose to demonstrate to the class. I was supposed to be a dancer who got too close. She put up her hands, while I stood there, with a serious look on my face, because I knew how important consent was. We learned it in Jean's class. When I saw her instant reaction with her hands, I danced away on my own, lightly, which produced some giggles from the others.

I realized that my shoulder felt better, thank goodness, but I was careful not to hurt it or do more stupid things. I'm so glad body parts tend to heal! I'll still be careful because we're going into our eighth week of dance now at school, and that's about halfway through the semester. I want to stay healthy so I can do yoga, swim, dance, and bike for the rest of my life. It's not worth the risk of getting injured again, because next time, it could be even more severe. We have our next 5Rhythms workshop this weekend, from Friday to Sunday, and I want to make sure I can do everything I want to do at the workshop. So, I'll be careful.

I also saw four people in our group who were dancing contact improv. Two had knee pads under their pants; I saw them. I'm pretty sure they go to the C.I. jams on Monday nights downtown. I'm looking forward to going soon, now that my eight-week mindfulness course is over, thank goodness.

If our university goes fully online for the rest of the semester, as it might because of the virus, then how will we have our dance classes? I bet the university doesn't plan for these kinds of things. I'd like to teach from home, personally, but I don't want to miss out on Jean's class. I'm now going to rest; I'm tired from so much dancing. I did a drawing in my dance sketchbook after today's session, too. It's fun and liberating to draw, as well as record my thoughts on paper through words. I feel like a kid again, with all my stick figures.

March 9th, 2020, Monday, Day 14

I danced today with several others. We practiced with our arms, hands, and the happy dance. It was nice to work with the other students (five or so), one at a time. Our homework was to teach someone either the happy dance, or the exercise we learned with our hands touching, or forearms catching. I taught my partner the happy dance, and hands touching, tonight during dinner.

Her first comment was, "This is really sensuous!" and I said, "Yes, I guess it is." And she said, "Do you only touch hands?" And I said, "No, we touch heads, backs, shoulders, hips, etc. On the ground, as well." She was in shock, I think, but she didn't seem to get jealous. She just said, "Like, guys and girls, or what?" I replied, "Guys and gals, gals and gals, guys and guys, etc. We all do it. Touching. Dancing. It's part of the class, and you get used to it." And I have, somewhat. But still it's a bit awkward, sometimes. It sure opens up my horizons, though.

We started out our class today with Jean's questioning the idea of contact, and the coronavirus that has hit the entire world. Susie spoke about it, too. I'm glad they did, because everyone was thinking about it, I'm sure. They decided to keep dancing, and we did too, because we showed up (eighteen or sixteen of us, I think). Some students were absent. We're trying to keep washing our hands, etc., but we are all touching each other in class. It's an essential part of the course.

Today I wondered again if we all went online and taught remotely, how would Jean teach our class? That would be sad. I'd probably be relieved for my classes—it's a lot of work to get to campus, and teach; it's grueling sometimes—but for her, so much of it is being with the students, sharing the space, listening, showing them how to move and 'be.' It wouldn't be the same online. Sure, we could read articles and watch videos, but it wouldn't be the same. So, I'll keep going until we have to stop.

Actually, I was so engrossed in the class today that I didn't write and hardly did the small dance (happy dance) on my own. I did the exercises with the others, and then we sat together in the closing circle, and I realized it must already be 12:20pm because students were filling the hallway with their chatter (as students always do) and rushing to their next class. We were still sitting in a circle and I needed to change my clothes, when Jean whispered to me, "It looks like you might be late to your midterm." I chuckled. "I think I might," I said. And I was four minutes late to my first class, so we only did one minute of 'settling in' (mindfulness practice), instead of the usual five that I offer the students at the start of all my classes. Oh well! It was a great way to begin my day, and I sweat a bit, too… Until Wednesday, I'll keep dancing!

March 12, 2020, Thursday, Day 15

It's with a very heavy heart that I write these words. I didn't know it yesterday, but I somehow sort of guessed that yesterday would be our last in-person dance class on campus this semester, and perhaps my last one ever on our campus, but I sincerely hope not. We were told late last night via email that all classes will be online starting next Friday, and we have Monday to Thursday next week to get prepared.

I'm in a state of shock: numb, feeling sad, yet also raw, like a lump of lead with a soft, sore spot in the middle. It's weird. I feel like something has died inside of me, like a close friend or loved one, and I'm trying to revive it, like one revives a broken car, and it keeps catching, then stopping, like a beating heart on its last breath. I know I'm overreacting, especially because this is 'just dance,' but dance has gotten me through a lot this last year, and this past half-semester on campus.

I was so ready to throw in the towel on teaching. I was frustrated. My eyes were tearing at the thought of having to drudge through it all for two more months, and yet dance got me through this rough patch, because I knew I could be light, and airy, and MYSELF. All I had to do was listen, and try to do what was asked of us, if I felt physically and mentally capable. And I did it. I got through eight weeks of the dance class, this high-risk class that my aunt, a former dancer, begged me not to take because she knew how high-risk it was. But I did it, and I was looking forward to every single class coming up for the next eight weeks. And now all that has shattered—my dream has unraveled at the seams.

I know I should be focusing on the three courses that I'm teaching instead, because I have to get them up and running online by next Friday, and I have two more classes to teach tomorrow. If anyone shows up, that is. But this is my precious dance journal, and I'm so indebted to its existence. I'm so glad to be able to express my thoughts, fears, and triumphs in its pages.

It's weird to think that someone else might read this journal because, up to now, it's 100% private and confidential, but I trust Jean as a teacher, and colleague, and maybe even friend. :) So, I'll let her read it, especially since it's part of our grade for this course. I'm trying to do all I can like the other students to fully participate and get the most out of this course. It's supposed to be research for my next book of fiction, but it's also research for me as a person: as an athlete, and as a social justice advocate and warrior!

I came across my ticket to our April dance event on campus and was very saddened by the fact that it will also be cancelled. I briefly wondered, "Will I get a refund?" and then I thought, "How insensitive and uncaring I am, worrying about my $6.50, or whatever it cost to purchase the ticket, when so many people are struggling right now because all these events have been cancelled due to the pandemic." It was a split-second thought, and the self-blame, guilt, and sadness still linger with me. I feel it in my body, and in my chest, right now as I watch the raindrops pound on the concrete outside my window and hear the pitter patter as they slap against the side of the wall. This weather goes really well with how I feel right now. Depressed. Unable to move into action.

I have about eighty more midterm papers to grade and a zillion emails to write, and yet I sit here drinking tea with milk next to my cat, who seems to have a bit of dementia and keeps crying out for more food, and wanting to go out to lick the wet leaves, because she thinks she's still in Belgium after eight years of living here. She's disoriented, especially at night, and I wonder if I'm not growing more like her every day during this crisis. I sit here with my tea, and my cat, watching the rain because I know how important it is to take the time to write in my dance journal and draw, which I will do when the rain calms and I can retrieve my sketchbook from the garage. I want to record what happened at our last class as best as I can recall—soon, before I forget all the important details that I want to be sure to save.

I don't know why I feel so passionate about recording all these details and doing this dance research. I truly don't. All I know is that I really, truly, need to record them, and experience the fullness of my being, as I explore dance, and my body, and my connection to others, and the earth. When I pay attention, time slows to a stillness, creating a softness inside of me that allows me to do this. It penetrates the core of my being.

For now, though, I'm just going to sit, breathe, and meditate to see what I need to do next. I hope Jean doesn't mind that I borrowed some of her words in her email announcement to our class this morning. I used it in my announcement to my classes, to let my students know that I'm here for them, and to keep breathing, and moving, etc. Her words were so well crafted; I didn't know how to say it better. I only used a sentence or two out of my whole huge message, so I hope she doesn't mind. I kind of guess she won't. If it were for a paper or public announcement, I would certainly have used quotes and proper APA citation. :)

March 25th, 2020, Wednesday, Day 16

We're in Week ten now, and for my classes, we had our first online remote session today from 12:30 to 2:20pm with Zoom. Last week was the week that students were supposed to have off while instructors like Jean, Susie, and I had to figure out how to move our courses to remote teaching. I wondered how Jean would do this, but she did a really good job. We logged in at 10:30am and we spoke on the screen together for a little bit. She asked us to share whatever we wanted with the group. I found it hard because we weren't muted and there was a baby/toddler crying, and birds chirping, etc., in the background.

Since I have ADHD, which I recently figured out, surprisingly, after spending fifty-five years on this planet, I realize how hard it is for me to concentrate when I have so many distractions around me, especially sounds. That's something I'm learning to deal with, and accept, now that I understand that my brain doesn't work like everyone else's. I don't have the natural filters that most people have, to keep my thoughts focused on one thing, despite all the sensory information coming in, a mile a minute, that distracts me so much.

When we moved afterwards, I was distracted by these noises, since I'm very sensitive to sounds, with my diagnosis of hyperacusis— *and ADHD*—but I tried not to let that ruin my experience. I wanted to hear all of Jean's guidance as we did small movements in our bedrooms, living rooms, offices, etc., but the child yelling/crying, and the birds chirping made it hard to hear her.

Luckily, when we shared afterwards, she had us mute our microphones and that was much better. I spoke twice at the beginning about the articles we'd read, and at the end, about taking care of Mom, moving outside, social distancing, etc. It was a good session and I think most of us felt relieved about meeting again after two weeks. Susie even proposed having a lunchtime chat sometime so people could check in with her.

While we did the small dance, I moved around on my yoga mat on the ground and felt empowered and strong. That was a relief. There are tensions everywhere because of this virus all over the world—I can feel them. So, this dancing can really help us, and me, especially, stay grounded during these challenging times of uncertainty and isolation, which also means lack of work, money, food, shelter, etc., for so many people.

Well, that's all for today. I'll continue writing in this dance journal, as Jean has asked us to do, and drawing in my sketchbook, and I'll try to do the small dance every day, as we're supposed to make movement and practice every day. I'd like to make mine the small dance, maybe five to ten minutes each morning, or when I feel stressed, like with the midterm I'm supposed to be running online in half an hour before my class. We'll see how that goes, but I did feel very balanced, like I was "riding on the surface of the earth," or the planet, as Jean asked us to do. It was like a dizzying, undulating wave—surfing the roundness, and remembering we're round, even when we stand on a flat surface, like the floor. Very powerful and important for survival!

DOING HAPPY DANCE AS MY OWN
PRACTICE FOR 5 OR 10 MINUTES
ALONE - STARTING THIS MORNING.

EYES
SEMI-
CLOSED

-NO COMPUTER   (NEW PRACTICE
-NO GROUP   ON MY OWN!)
-ONLY ME
(W/ KITTY WATCHING, AND PARTNER
WATCHING) EATING BREAKFAST)
LOOKING OUT AT BUDDHA + PLANTS
IN GARDEN. AT TREES. SUNSHINE
SOFTNESS OF HEART. ROUNDNESS
OF BODY / THOUGHTS. LEARNING
← CARPET PATIENCE, SLOWING DOWN.

Day 18   HURT FOOT / ANKLE

YIKES!

STRETCHING + ICING BOTTOM OF
FOOT + CALF MUSCLES AFTER
TOO MUCH WALKING FAST W/o
PROPER   WARM-UP.

PLANTAR FASCIITIS (sp). IS BACK.
SPRAINED ANKLE, TOO. DAMN!)

PAIN!!   TAKING CARE OF MY
          BODY IS IMPERATIVE
BOARD   RIGHT NOW. FORCES
        ME TO SLOW DOWN.!!
← STEP I WARMED UP ALL OF
MY LEGS / FEET BEFORE DOING THE
HAPPY DANCE TODAY AND MY FEET (+
BODY + BRAIN) WERE HAPPIER! :)

Day 19

STILL HURT FOOT. DARN! IT KILLS. I NEED TO ICE IT WHILE DOING HAPPY DANCE (+ WINCING AT PAIN)

REALIZED NAME OF MY MEMOIR: "HAPPY DANCE" TODAY,

5-10 MINUTES TUNING-IN SURFING-RIDING- THE WAVES OF MY FEET. ME, HAPPY, THINKING OF BOOK, AND ITS TITLE.

SWAYING MOVING MEDITATING TO PIANO MUSIC

SAKURA, OUR KITTY SNORING ZZZ

ALIVE!

4 POTTED PLANTS (peeing nt)

CALM

PEACE FUL

BUT

OUCH!!!

Day 20

DOING 5 RHYTHMS AT HOME VIA ZOOM W/ PARTNER

FOOT IS BETTER, THANK GOODNESS!

LIGHTER

SAD FOR A FRIEND

TENSION IN PARTNER

about space, music, walking, etc. closed up in tight quarters new for 21+ days - not easy. NOT smooth sailing.

DOING HAPPY DANCE TO FLOWING + STILLNESS

ZOOM

LEDGE COMPUTER

KITTY

LESS PAIN W/ SHOES

NOT SAME AS DANCING IN PERSON. + (GOOD FRIEND + HAS COVID-19)

DID FOOT MASSAGE ON SELF YESTERDAY + HELPED!

Sketchbook, Days 17 to 20

*M*arch 26th, 2020, Thursday, Day 17

I'm doing my homework alone, as Jean asked us to do every day. I've decided to do the happy dance for five to ten minutes in front of our tiny patio, as I remain inside, looking out the window at the palm tree, tiny green bushes, our Buddha statue, Kwan Yin statuette, birds, etc. I'm also looking inside myself, feeling the earth, grounding myself, noticing the roundness of my tiny movements. My partner was watching me as she ate breakfast, and so was my cat, Sakura. She was doing her happy dance on her soft cushion as she does all day long (she's sixteen). Sometimes, I'd like to be her and be lazy and simply purr and wait for dinner, or wait to be petted, and bask in the sunshine and do nothing else but ponder the world.

I think that's what I'll do. I'll be a cat and do my happy dance all day long. I'll remain immobile, then I'll be stretching, and waiting for dinner, for kind family members to feed me. It sure beats teaching, especially this online teaching, which is super hard to do when exams crash, like yesterday, and grades don't show up, like today.

I need to be balanced and sure of myself in this world of uncertainty, and scarcity, in so many ways. I want to continue to help others, and to do so I need to keep optimistic, positive, and centered. The slowing down, happy dance, and guidance from Jean, and observing all that surrounds me—and within me—will keep it all going. I have to trust that it will. I did a little drawing, as usual, in my sketchbook. It's Day 17, my first day without formal instruction. It's time to move on. Time to move. Time to *be*, really *be*, in the moment. This is my happy dance.

March 27th, 2020, Friday, Day 18

I'm in the moment all right! I have planter fasciitis, which I had several years ago, and it was super painful and debilitating. I wasn't careful when I went walking fast yesterday, as I've been doing every morning for two weeks since we've been forced to stay at home because of COVID-19. I went down my usual hill in my new sports shoes, and it felt like my feet were thumping and stomping harder than usual. I was trying to get my heart rate up and break into a sweat to lower my LDL cholesterol, which is too high, and my fasting glucose, which keeps creeping up on me. It's all genetic, and not my fault, all of this, my doctor keeps saying. And I suppose I was trying to get it over with because I had so much to do yesterday, with all my teaching, etc.

I felt pain in my ankle and at the bottom of my left foot. I've felt this pain before during these past few days, especially upon waking up. Of course, I ignored it, wishing it would just go away on its own. Well it didn't, and today, I can't wish it away anymore. It's too painful. So, I googled what to do and watched three physical therapists—all in very different outfits and styles of instruction, quite amazing, really—for twenty-five minutes as they described how to get rid of it in three to five minutes. Really? What a miracle! So, I tried *all* of their remedies and then went for a slow walk without hills around the block.

There's nothing like pain to slow you down and make you conscious of your body parts, right? I tried to turn inward, like I did with the happy dance this morning. I wonder, is it cheating if I listen to music as I do it? Music makes me really happy a lot of the time, if it fits my needs; I'm also aware that it's aligning my various chakras while I'm doing nothing. Kind of cool. Anyway, I did the small dance *after* my huge warm-up: ankles, calves, and bottoms of my feet, and that was beneficial. I hope I learned my lesson. Then I iced the sole of my foot after my little walk.

One article said to bike or swim. Well, I can't do *that* because all the pools are closed, so I cleaned off the cobwebs on my trusty bike that I bought as a grad student in Japan, the one I rode for so many years in Brussels every day, and haven't touched here in several years. Why is it that our American society is so averse to public transportation and biking to get to the store, work, gym, etc.? I didn't want to get killed, like roadkill, that's why I let my bike rot in the garage. But now it's time to take it out for a spin, since most cars are parked in their driveways for the time being. So, it's much safer to exercise. I wonder if I can do the happy dance while pedaling? I'll try.

March 28th, 2020, Saturday, Day 19

I decided that this will all be a book about dancing and mindful movement, about navigating space and gravity, about looking inward and connecting with others. It's about improvisation, contact, and no contact, like right now, and survival skills for coping with and navigating unknown waters. Like tacking when sailing—it all depends on the wind, and the skill of the sailor, or captain of the vessel. We are all captains of our own vessels, and right now, we're in unchartered territory, in the perfect storm. I see it here at our living room table, while sipping my morning tea, and it's already 1:15pm. What is this new normal? Our body clocks are messed up, and we're off balance.

I just called my brother, who said he was having breakfast with his family an hour ago. He sounded embarrassed, and I said, "Don't worry, I just finished mine." Everything is askew, and it's all unexpected. Doing the happy dance prepares me to move into this world from a vantage point. I feel more solid, and grounded, with more spaciousness, as I surf the slippery slope of the choppy waters up ahead. I was doing this after spending fifteen minutes on my feet.

Yep, my planter fasciitis is worse now, probably because I've admitted that I have it. I stretched, kneaded, pulled, rolled, etc., my Achilles tendons, calf muscles, and planter surface of my feet— my underbelly, if you will—and then went for a walk around the block. I moved slowly, carefully, while avoiding others through social distance (we're all doing this now, thankfully), while on the phone with my brother. But now, back home, it's flaring up again. Damn. I feel like the more careful I am, the more it flares up and hurts. Sharp pain comes in bursts. Of course, I'm glad it's not something way worse, like cancer, but it's still really annoying.

For extra support, I decided to keep my shoes on inside, instead of wearing my slippers, like I always do. I hope this won't hurt my back like it did after I left Japan, after six years of wearing slippers everywhere, when I finally put on shoes again in Belgium. Once, I forgot, and took the train into town to my workplace in the heart of Brussels. I was wearing a business suit and pink, fluffy slippers. It was raining and they got muddy. Everyone on the train thought I was crazy, or sick, and they stared at me as if I'd escaped from a mental hospital. I had to duck into a shoe store before going to work to buy a new pair of shoes. Nobody in the store wanted to serve me either, due to those slippers of mine.

Anyway, I'm in my sneakers now. My tea's growing cold and I just did the happy dance after planting four pots of vegetables. Luckily, my organic seeds arrived last night. I'm still waiting for the planter to arrive today, so I can plant them all. :)

While doing the happy dance and looking at my patio, and my four new pots, I got a great idea. This book, this memoir, about dance and how it's affected my life this year, will be called, "Happy Dance." Why not? When I do this dance, this practice, I'm tuned in, and it makes me grounded, spacious, full of breath, and optimism. And I'm happy. Many people—no, all people right now in this world—need happiness to brighten their days. Maybe this book will brighten their days. They're shut in and can't go outside. Or maybe they're less fortunate and have nowhere to go. Maybe they live in the streets and have no shelter, food, or water, let alone the hand sanitizer, wipes, or toilet paper that none of us can get, of course, right now.

So, I'll write this book for everyone, to inspire, guide, and encourage people to do the happy dance for survival in unknown waters, or in the perfect storm, like now, with COVID-19. I'll keep writing every day, and I hope I don't get in trouble with Jean, because it's supposed to be only about dance, I suppose, yet the happy dance covers so much more. I don't think she'll mind, really. She's super cool, and if it serves others, especially our students, she'll be fine with it, I'm sure. Who's going to type it all up? Guess it'll be me! Hard to believe it's spring break!

March 29th, 2020, Sunday, Day 20

What a spring break, right? Not like I usually spend it. Last year, I was in Japan, practicing my Japanese. Now, I'm in self isolation, with my partner and kitty, and doing everything online. I'm growing— well, planting, at least—seeds for produce, and waiting for delivery stuff to come so we can try to eat normally and healthily. I'm a vegetarian again, maybe out of want, maybe out of need, because we can't get fish, chicken, or meat at the moment. I'm supposed to do a blood test mid-April, and I doubt I'll be able to do it now. That's probably better, because I had some wine yesterday. Only two small glasses, but it's too much sugar for my system.

And now I have a stye in my eye, and I'm waiting for the nurse to call me back about that. At least my foot is feeling better, thank goodness. I'm wearing my shoes with implants inside our condo now, to keep my feet supported, and I stretch my calves and Achilles tendons every hour or so. What luxury! I have the impression that I'm doing nothing most of the time, but time is still going by.

A good friend has COVID-19, and she's younger than me. I want to write her back and offer support, but I don't know what to say. She's in Brussels. My partner and I have talked about possibly relocating back to Brussels. We've been here eight years, and we both work really hard. It's so expensive to live in California, and it's especially difficult to stay at home during the pandemic. We're both getting really stir crazy.

Luckily, my office is in the bedroom, where it's been for five to six years, so we're both used to working from home. But now, our place seems so much smaller, like the walls are closing in on us, because we can't really leave, except to go on our daily, or twice-daily walks, or get the mail from the mailbox. And I have to sanitize each envelope, my hands, the doorknobs, the key, etc., each time I get the mail. It's such a pain. But it's necessary, with so many people getting sick.

A stye in the eye is super painful, but I bet all these people getting coronavirus would trade places with me in a heartbeat. Jean did a great job posting dance resources/life resources in our online course before spring break. I've been messaging my students a lot lately, to reassure them, but now, I'm trying to give them (and me) a break. It's a well-needed break, believe me. Self-care is super important, I've found, along with adequate sleep, water, and good, healthy food.

Luckily, I took many macrobiotic cooking classes in Belgium: Indian, Italian, Italian again, French, etc. I even taught cooking in Japan: Belgian and Mexican cooking. I'm happy in the kitchen, peeling, chopping, simmering, etc. I especially like to eat afterwards, and if I can get organic grains, spices, and produce, that's the best. At the moment, though, I'll take what I can get, which is turning into slim pickings, unfortunately.

I did the happy dance today as part of our weekly Sunday 5Rhythms online class. This is the third week that we've participated with the group. It's short, only forty-five minutes, so we started dancing thirty minutes beforehand, which made it better. But now I'm exhausted, and all I want to do is lie down, sleep, or read. Yet my stye is still hurting, and even itching, which might mean it's healing, who knows?

I think because it's Sunday I deserve to lie down and relax as I wait for the nurse to call back. That's self-care. I'm listening to spa music, and trying to enjoy the peace and quiet, which comes so rarely here, with loud neighbors on both sides of our thin walls. And I should be doing all this other work piled on my desk, but instead, I'm going to do my happy dance lying down and reading that novel I started three weeks ago.

Today, I planted four more plants and that was tiring, so... Oh well, one day, this will pass. And when it does, we'll all have learned a big lesson. At least I hope so! Those of us who are still around, that is. It's so sad, what's happening in Spain, New York City, Italy, China, etc. Wow. Who would've thought? Dance teaches survival, and we're now in survival mode. I feel rather lucky to have a place to live...

Day 21

Doing happy dance as a silent meditation afternoon / dance to get out tension/stress

SMILE! I AM

STILLNESS

SILENCE SEE IN EYE BETTER

LEARNING TO LOOK WITHIN AS I STAND, EYES CLOSED

+ SWAY SWAYING W/ WORLD, SURFING ON EARTH'S FLAT SURFACE

DID SOME JIGGING + JINGLING AND NOW I'M MORE RELAXED, CENTERED +

FEELING UNDULATIONS IN KNEES

DON'T NEED MUSIC TO DANCE!

GROUNDED

DON'T NEED TO DANCE TO DANCE!!

FOOT BETTER (W/SHOES NOW!)

DISCOVERY OF SELF

Day 22

SHAKING FIRST

STILLNESS AGAIN!

BIRDS CHIRPING KEE KEE KEE

SHAKE IT OUT!

CLOUDY DAY

ALL STOPS. JUST LISTEN.

YEAH!

SOOTHING MUSIC

SPRING BREAK RESEARCH DAY

KOYO LEAVES, GREEN (TENDER)

- NEED TO DO TAXES TODAY
- NEED TO DO HAPPY DANCE MORE!

iPAD

SMOOTH RELAXING

I AM ONE

BEAUTIFUL JAPANESE TREE

SOFTNESS, CLARITY, WISDOM

o o /s Sunny day!

Day 23

stye in eye (1 week!)

Doing happy dance w/hurt shoulders / upper back tension + eye still w/ stye in it.

upper back pain

HAPPY DANCE
SWAYING
FEELING
LISTENING
WAITING

SUNNY DAY - SPRING BREAK - TAXES STILL NOT DONE

Sipping tea afterward to write + draw in dance journal.

Mild rotation of legs, feet on floor w/socks on

Time seems to stop. Had scare last night. Hot neck, dry cough, chest constriction. Took allergy medicine + it all went away!

foot better ☺

Do uncharted waters for all of us. Trying to keep afloat.

BALANCE + MOVEMENT HEY.

Day 24

music

SUNNY W/ CLOUDS

PALM TREE IN WIND

CALM OUTSIDE, NO CARS AGITATED INSIDE (ME)

WANTING TO DANCE MORE, WANTING TO GET OUT. SHOP, EAT, SIP TEA — BUT CAN'T.

SADNESS — LOSS — SO MANY PEOPLE FALLING ILL, SO MANY DEATHS. FEELING POWERLESS. AT LEAST I CAN CONTROL MY LIFE (I THINK)

SOUNDS OF PALM TREES RUSTLING, NEIGHBOR SHOUTING AT HER KIDS, BIRDS CHIRPING (THEY'RE HAPPY AT LEAST) — MAYBE I'M LOSING WEIGHT? (NO MEAT, CHICKEN OR FISH —) LISTENING TO CLASSICAL MUSIC + PONDERING MY LIFE — HAPPY DANCE IS WORKING MIRACLES!

Sketchbook, Days 21 to 24

$\mathscr{M}$arch 30th, 2020, Monday, Day 21

What a spring break. It's calmer now, with the zillions of kids next door studying part of the day, then yelling the rest of the time. I'm starting to notice more things as I slow down. I notice that the half yogurt I just ate—actually, a quarter of it, because it's my first one in two weeks, and I only have one—well, I've noticed it doesn't sit well with me. It feels heavy on my gut, and I only put a few tiny spoonfuls into my mouth. I also noticed my tongue puckering up, like it's acidic or burning, and normally vanilla yogurt doesn't do that to me. So, I'll not eat the other half because it's probably rotten. It was delivered like that to us on Saturday. Too bad. But this is a fresh learning experience. I'm learning to slow down, and to taste that what I no longer tasted: air, water, yogurt, even emotions.

Some tastes are sweet, like my mom's orange that I picked from her tree on Tuesday (at a socially acceptable distance of eight feet). And other things are sour, or heavy, like this yogurt, or even the chicken that my mom and I had on our packaged Caesar chicken salads. I hadn't had chicken in two and a half weeks, and it tasted heavy, like fowl—it was foul—but it tasted strong and heavy, and even greasy on my tongue. I ate it because Mom bought it for me, but it didn't sit well in my body. My stomach bloated that afternoon and evening; I think there were hormones in it. Yuck.

So, doing the happy dance every day, and being forced to stay in—except to get essentials like groceries, which we're not doing at all, or going to the hospital, which we don't have to do yet either, thank God, or exercising outside by walking two to three times a day—is forcing me to slow down, look inside, and appreciate what *is*.

I feel the time sliding by and that makes me sad because I like living in the present. It's like noticing grains of sand falling through my fingers most of the time. The more I grasp and try to hold on, the more I try to 'seize the moment,' and 'capture' it, the more I notice it leaving… slipping through my fingers… and I feel a sense of deep loss. I keep thinking I should be accomplishing so much right now: taking time to help others, achieve my goals, prepare my courses, respond to emails, search for a new job, etc.

These thoughts are constantly running in my head, yet I know that all that can wait. It *needs* to wait, because I'm on a path to self-discovery. I've boarded that train that has my name on it; I need to fasten my seat belt, lean back, and enjoy the ride. I need to look out the window and take in the scenery whizzing past. I need to sip my tea in silence and really taste the tea leaves for once, and the sweet milk that's in my cup. Cup after cup after cup. Because I know that maybe one day soon, perhaps even next week, I will have no more milk to put in my cup. I'll have tea though, luckily. I stocked up before we even knew about COVID-19, and I'll have hot water, assuming we can continue to pay the bills. But I may not enjoy my milky tea for long.

That's why it's important to make each moment last as long as possible. This sounds trite, like a cliché, but it isn't. It's the key to happiness, the key to living fully with what is. And in this fullness, in this glimpse of what is—what is real around us and inside of us—we can have hope. Life is shattering down around us right now, with fear, sickness, worry, and death. And hope is what will keep us all afloat, along with swift action.

So, by remaining in the present and settling here on my sofa each day, with my teapot of milky tea and my cat purring next to me—begging to be caressed yet again behind her soft ears—and writing in my dance journal, I hope to move the world. I hope to shift people's vantage point by allowing them to grant themselves the opportunity—like I am right now –to slow down, relax, treasure the moment, that unique thought, that unexpected pause on 'play,' and experience what *is* right now, while we are in the midst of this global health crisis.

It's like our friend's nephew, who's from Bogotá, Colombia, said to us via Zoom on Saturday, in Spanish: "The earth has reset its settings. It's done 'control, alt, delete.'" He's right. It's time for us to pick up and go in an entirely new direction; a direction of caring about others, about this earth and *all* living beings, not only humans, and especially about caring for ourselves in this very special and sacred time. The happy dance is transporting me there, and so is this journal. We'll see what comes next. Tune in!

March 31st, 2020, Tuesday, Day 22

It's both spring break and Cesar Chavez day, so there's less traffic, less work, and less frenzy in our neighborhood. It's peaceful and silent, and our kitty, Sakura, is snoozing, as usual. I just did my happy dance and I've realized how important it is to start my working day off with it each morning. I only do about five minutes or so, along with a few minutes of shaking and boogieing my whole body beforehand to warm up. It's amazing how this daily practice, which would certainly seem unusual to some people, makes me feel more rested, peaceful, and alive.

This morning, I went for a walk and found some nice branches in the trash with sweet-smelling flowers on them. I was careful to wash my hands afterwards, after planting them in our big pot out front that was previously housing a huge weed. Then, during my happy dance, I got inspiration and tied the branches to a plastic pole I had stuck in another pot of flowers inside. We'll see if that helps support the branches as they spread their roots in the soil. I'm planting a lot lately, and even trying hydroponics—with carrot ends, green onion ends, and lettuce—in two small pots of water. The carrots and onions are taking hold, but the lettuce is just turning brown, like an ugly scab, and a wet one at that. I'll keep it up for a few more days and then try something else. Maybe round onions will work, too. Who knows?

I'm not usually a gardener, but it's time to get more creative and resourceful, now that we can't go to the store or seem to order what we want online. All deliveries are impossible at the moment. They are overwhelmed at all the online shopping sites and major grocery stores for produce, rice, milk, toilet paper, etc. We'll see if we get the weekly delivery that my partner ordered from local farmers. We got our first one on Saturday, three hours late. And the yogurt was spoiled. But that's all right. At least it was a good attempt at getting protein.

I'm realizing that this is a nice time for reflection, for pacing ourselves, slowing down, and realizing what is essential in life. We're all given twenty-four hours per day, and it's up to us to decide where and how we'll use this time. If we don't, decisions will be made for us, and opportunities will pass us by. Now some people might prefer that all decisions be made for them, like when they were kids, because it's easier to just be a follower and obey the status quo. But others, like me, fade in the sun when we're put to no good use. If I just lie there like a crèpe, basking in the sun, doing nothing, I will wither. I need to know that I'm being useful, that I'm using my resources and talents to help others grow, like my little seedlings, and that I'm learning and growing myself.

Life is a process, a damn hard process at times. But we need to sit still—and stand somewhat still, like in the happy dance every day—and really tune into our thoughts, emotions, and physical sensations, these feelings that overcome us for no reason sometimes. They can transport us to new levels—unconscious levels of awareness—if we'll just be more open to their whispers of advice.

Tapping into this complex garden—this complex array of thoughts and emotions that have been planted in our bodies and minds since we were born, and rarely used, takes skill and talent. We need to cultivate this skill and talent, like a gardener—like me, right now—cultivates their garden: one seedling at a time. And this garden needs patience, awareness, and attention to let the sunshine, water, rich soil, and air bring it to fruition. Then the seeds will reap beautiful harvests.

We have to trust this process as well as our own inner wisdom. The happy dance is grounding me, and leading me on this path of awareness, so I can then share its fruits with the world, like my carrots one day!

April 1ˢᵗ, 2020, Wednesday, Day 23, April fool's day

Time seems to have slowed down so much that it's literally stopped. I play gentle, relaxing, soothing music all day, while my partner wants the more modern, cooler, jazzier, faster stuff. But that kind of music makes my heart beat too fast, and my ears ring, so I ask her to slow it down and soften it, like sweet butter churning to get solid. Too fast and it creates hard, lumpy, rock-like formations—cliffs inside the bucket. Slower, churning, meditative movements with intention and precision, but not yet perfectionistic precision, just careful, attentive precision, makes the butter come out smooth and sweet.

I've realized that life is like this music: slowing down, doing the happy dance in the morning. Heck, why not do it several times per day? It can reset the switch of time and keep us in movement and balance, and provide trust in the earth, boosting our synchronicity with the planet's rhythms. It holds us in the flow and energy of what's around us and helps keep us tuned into reality. Not the kind of reality that one watches on TV, or the news—that is horrific most of the time and incites fear. The kind of reality that teaches us the pulsations of life that flow through nature and all the planet's gifts to us that go constantly unnoticed through our human condition. This condition, like a fungus or disease, is our constant business—our need to get things done at all costs—which brings a high price to pay for ourselves, our health, our livelihoods, and certainly our planet's natural resources.

Slowing down and being present in all moments of the day and evening—because day and evening is all the same, it's in these twenty-four hour periods, which are human-made to begin with—teaches us to live, be, recuperate, flow, and pulsate with life all around us. It's in the trees, bushes, oceans, insects, wind, mountains, grass, flowers… even in the dust that accumulates at our feet.

We neglect the essential parts of living through this drive and determination to succeed, always succeed, and be at the top of our game. But what a dangerous game we've invented for ourselves: striving to win, combat, accumulate power, prestige, and wealth, and in doing so, depleting the source of richness that we have been given through our very existence.

The happy dance can teach us to let go; letting go of this drive to always succeed and become the best—proving to others that we are the best—and let others rot in the process, because after all, who cares about them? They don't have as much drive, energy, resources, or power as we do, so let's just let them rot by the road and 'keep on trucking.'

Yeah, 'just do it.' In our actions, we are what we do, just like, 'we are what we eat.' Because our motivation as humans is to do, climb, win, and succeed. We do this, then we suffer the consequences directly from our actions: not seeing, not feeling, not noticing that what surrounds us. Missing out on these precious moments of time, which pass like a click of the fingers—instantly—and we succumb to numbing ourselves with food, drink, drugs, sex, passive entertainment… with TV, videos, video games, chats, social media, music, etc.

We may seem as if we're living, but are we really here? Are we really home in ourselves? Are we tuned into life as it really exists? How can we find out? By being present with what is, with what surrounds us, and especially by listening, feeling, and tuning into our essential human nature, through our body, mind, and spirit. I'm going to do this happy dance several times per day and see if it keeps me tuned in. I like this channel. I'll keep it in my favorites. Damn, I hope all that I'm writing each day in this journal isn't gibberish. It's what I feel and know, and I desperately want to share it with the world. Hopefully, one day I'll get that chance!

April 2nd, 2020, Thursday, Day 24

Each day seems to blend into the next. I've established my own little rhythm, my new normal, my new 'now' style of living, where I get adequate sleep (seven to eight hours), which I haven't had since I was... actually I don't think I've *ever* had adequate sleep. My parents fought a lot, and spoke in loud whispers, in the room next to me when I was growing up, so I didn't sleep very much. Maybe as a baby/toddler? I wonder. Probably not, because my big brother used to tease and pretty much torture me all the time.

It's interesting, getting enough sleep now, really interesting. My brain works way better. Thoughts are smoother and come more readily. They always came, but I was bombarded by them, without a systematic and logical order. I was attacked, like machine gunfire, most of the time, with all these barbaric thoughts about how to improve my life, my financial situation, my status, my well-being, and guess what? None of these nifty ideas worked.

My mom's cousin used to say something interesting at the dinner table while looking at me. I think she took pity on me, considering all those efforts I made to get ahead. She'd say, "if you throw enough shit against the wall, then something's bound to stick." She's a sweet woman, but I swear, those were her exact words. So how am I supposed to truly benefit from life's pleasures and treasures if I've been skipping around bits of doggy doo, or actually swimming in it, for my entire existence? Impossible!

So, now that I've taken a step back, a first step back, to reflect on my fifty-five years of existence, I've gotten a huge shock by realizing that my life, and its foundation, was built on sandcastles made of poop. Am I going crazy? I wonder. Mental illness flows like lava in my family. It could be that. But I'd wager to guess (is that the same thing?) that I'm finally figuring out my ADHD (Attention-Deficit Hyperactivity Disorder), and my way of dealing with it, through this forced introspection, this forced hibernation at home, this forced wellness, and sleeping, and eating right, and getting lots of exercise outside. And nature appreciation. I take lots of pictures of flowers, trees, mountains, and insects, and write little captions about them, and send one a day out into the world on Instagram and Facebook as an author—using my pseudonym for the lesbian romance novels that I write—not as the real me, of course.

The real me doesn't do social media, except for maintaining a very passive and lukewarm LinkedIn presence. The real me doesn't like to be exposed to the public eye, so I hide behind the author, who is still me, but writing under another name. She's younger, more hip, more tech savvy, and much more popular with readers and the global crowd. The real me is an academic trying to make a living teaching university students about life and global issues, intercultural communication, and formerly, business management from a global perspective, until I was thrown out of more than one college, mind you, for either being a lesbian—outed by one of my former bosses, without my consent—or for being a woman, or getting better course evaluations, and researching more than the others, who were paid three times more than me for doing a third of the work.

Anyway, that's all in the past. What I'm realizing now is that only the present moment (NOW) counts, as Eckhart Tolle, the author of *The Power of Now*, says. I highly respect his work. All this reflecting on past wounds, and the future, strategizing to get a better job, more money, more prestige, more fame, success, and all those fake friends who come with success—well—it's all dog poop. Piles of it. Yep, I'm tired of slinging it against the wall.

I'm going to slow down, sip my tea, listen to the classical music on my iPad, do the happy dance, sleep more, eat better, slow down on the wine—we never really exaggerated, but it's not that great for you. All sugar, isn't it?—exercise more, be in harmony with nature, pets, insects, animals of all kinds, and especially, others, like my partner, my family, friends, colleagues… Even those I don't know yet or don't particularly care for, like our homophobic, male chauvinist, disrespectful neighbor who won't talk to us, or even look at us, when we say "hi."

It's not easy to be in harmony with someone like that, but I try not to take his aggressive attitude seriously. He actually threatened me last summer, telling me how terrible of a person I was, and when he approached me in the parking lot with his fists ready to strike, I braced for the worst. He was going to hit me. Luckily, his kids jumped out of his car, yelling that they'd miss their flight back to the East Coast, and got him to leave me alone. Anyway, I'll try to be in harmony with all living beings, and especially with myself, and with the PRESENT MOMENT, because that's all we have, and all we'll ever have. I'm finally realizing that it's enough, more than enough, if we can only appreciate its fullness and beauty.

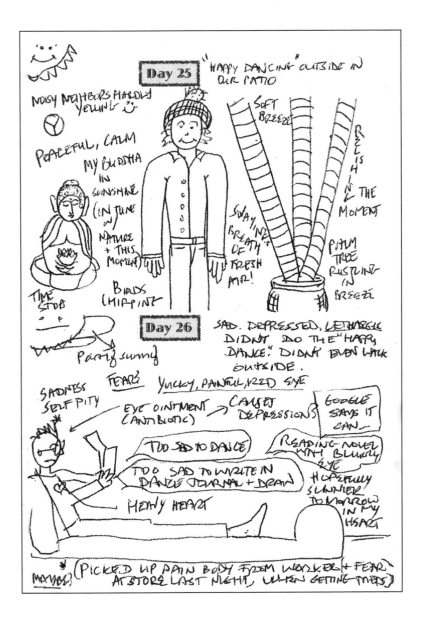

Day 25 — "HAPPY DANCING" OUTSIDE IN OUR PATIO

NOISY NEIGHBORS HARDLY YELLING ☺

PEACEFUL, CALM

MY BUDDHA IN SUNSHINE (IN JUNE & NATURE + THIS MOMENT)

SOFT BREEZE

RELISHING THE MOMENT

SWAYING BREATH OF FRESH AIR!

PALM TREE RUSTLING IN BREEZE

TIME STOP

BIRDS CHIRPING

Day 26 — SAD. DEPRESSED, LETHARGIC. DIDN'T DO THE "HAPPY DANCE." DIDN'T EVEN WALK OUTSIDE.

Partly sunny

SADNESS SELF PITY

FEAR!

YUCKY, PAINFUL, RED EYE

EYE OINTMENT (ANTIBIOTIC) → CAUSES DEPRESSION?

GOOGLE SAYS IT CAN...

TOO SAD TO DANCE

READING NOVEL WITH BLURRY EYE

TOO SAD TO WRITE IN DANCE JOURNAL + DRAW

HOPEFULLY SUNNIER TOMORROW IN MY HEART

HEAVY HEART

MAYBE? * (PICKED UP PAIN BODY FROM WORKER + FEAR AT STORE LAST NIGHT, WHEN GETTING MEDS)

IT'S A MUCH BETTER DAY, SO FAR. LUCKILY! I HEAR
BIRDS CHIRPING ... MY MOOD IS MUCH BETTER.

Day 27

I WANT TO DANCE + WRITE
AND BE HERE (NOT LIKE
YESTERDAY). COULD IT BE
THAT I ATE A BAGEL
INSTEAD OF OATMEAL FOR
BREAKFAST YESTERDAY?

MUSIC

EYE

5
RHYTHMS
WAVE

STACCATO!

FEELING
BETTER

GETTING OUT MY
ANGER + SADNESS

MOVING ... GYRATING ... SWINGING
TO THE 5 RYTHMS WITH
OUR (NOW) ONLINE ZOOM
CLASS TODAY ... THE 3RD
SINCE THE CRISIS ...

MOVING FROM CONFUSION
+ FRUSTRATION TO
TRUST + STILLNESS

(Journaling furiously today helped)

eye stye

Day 28

chilly

RAINY, COLD DAY

HAPPY DANCE
(Doesn't look like it, though).

Feeling small + insignificant

cat asleep

Partner in bad
mood a lot —
not easy.

EMAILS.
CONCERNED
STUDENTS.
OVERLOAD.

Big load on my shoulders.
I liked spring Break better.
(Even though it's my
journey to healing)

Not smooth
Sailing —
Feeling
guilty for
taking time to
write in dance
journal.

Sketchbook, Days 25 to 28

April 3rd, 2020, Friday, Day 25

I decided to venture outside on the patio to do my happy dance this morning. It's 70 degrees Fahrenheit, so it's warmer outside than inside our condo, where it's 68 degrees. I was afraid I'd be really bothered by the noisy neighbors and I wouldn't be able to concentrate. Worse yet, I was afraid I'd sabotage what I've been doing by getting angry and frustrated with those around me, who are also cooped up in their homes. On the other side of us, sharing a wall, are a zillion kids and their loud mom, and all the cars whizzing by on our busy street. But I'm happy, nonetheless.

I'm relieved to report that it's not too cold out here, even with wet hair. I washed it after my walk this morning and I'm wearing a beanie cap for warmth and an extra jacket. Besides, it's pleasant to hear the palm trees rustle in the wind. I don't know if it's technically one or three palm trees. They share the same base and roots, but the base splits into three trunks that aim toward the sky. All the leaves come together at the top and rustle over my head in the wind. And a few planes have gone over, which is rare, and some cars have sped by, but not like before the stay-at-home order. It used to be nonstop traffic and now, there's one car every few seconds or so, which is much better for meditating, journaling, and doing the happy dance outdoors.

My drawing was different today, too. Until today, I was drawing myself inside our place: the whole figure of me, adding more and more details each day, but my posture only stayed slightly the same. I had written lots of words around my figure and it's been very crowded on the page. Then today, now that I'm outside in nature, more or less—there's still concrete on the ground, and behind and in front of me, with the stucco walls of our small patio—but I'm under our potato tree, too, which I love. It's sacred; it really is.

My yoga teacher gave me Tibetan flags from real Tibetan monks, who brought them to her from Tibet. I decorated the tree with them, and now they're fading, but sacred. And we had three glass hearts that my partner bought from a very kind woman in Mexico in January. We tied them to the tree with matching blue, pink, and peach silk ribbons when we got home. And I have chimes from India that need to be polished, which hang from one of the branches, and a small statue of Kwan Yin holding a little precious bottle. She sits nestled in the grass under the tree at my feet.

But the most interesting and sacred part of this tree, which gives us dark purple flowers nearly year-round, is that a branch broke off at the top about six months ago, and it's suspended upside down. The part of the branch that should have died never did, and it's flowering again, with fresh, tender green leaves, as if its branch had never split. That's a miracle. That's why we call it our magic potato tree.

It's hard to understand what we cannot understand as humans, but the energy and love still flow through that tree, and through that broken, wounded branch, allowing it to flourish. We humans can be like this too—resilient, strong, flourishing. We just need the time, faith, and willpower to heal and know that everything will be all right in the end.

Things look bleak right now for everyone in this world, but I know we'll get through this as a human race, all together, and we'll be much stronger for it afterwards. So, with our planet, which has been suffering so much due to human waste, human recklessness, and greed, I hope everyone right now can take the time to turn inward, like me, and learn to do the happy dance inside or outside, or wherever they may be.

And I wish we can all come together soon—very soon—when the time is right, and turn this world around, with nature on our side, instead of treating it like the enemy, like so many of us have been doing, especially big business. I wish we could make it all right again, with renewed health, energy, compassion, hope, optimism, care, and love for all. That's what I wish.

April 3rd, 2020, Friday afternoon, Day 25 continued

The happy dance is turning into the slow dance!

April 5th, 2020, Sunday, Day 27

Friday was great. I wrote a thought later in the afternoon about how my world, and that of so many others, is slowing down. Perhaps this new normal, and my book, should be called "slow dance," instead of "happy dance"? I'd add that a slow dance can be an expression of love between two people who really care for each other, or it could be a very awkward time for one or two persons who are kind of thrown into unexpected circumstances.

I have really bad memories of slow dancing with men and women, and very awkward, embarrassing feelings, conversations, and movements that occurred during these dances—if you can call them dances. Stepping on toes, sweaty hands, bad breath, whispers of weird conversations, misunderstandings, even shaking, and boredom. I should write a book about those experiences, or at least a short story, sometime. It might get a few laughs.

Yesterday was April 4th, Day 26, and I woke up in a sad and depressed mood. It was before breakfast, while I was meditating. I did an exercise in one of the books that I'm reading, "The Call: Discovering why we're here," by Oriah Mountain Dreamer. It's a great book, and the third that I've read by her this year. She goes deep, really deep, and I think she and I have a ton in common, in many ways. She's also searching for the stillness within, in a spiritual way, through movement, and non-movement, and non-doing. She's really listening to the call, the invitation, the dance within, and nature. These are the names of her books. In fact, I bought "The Dance" at a book sale at our local library because I loved the cover—an image of a woman dancing in a red dress; I was intrigued, and that's how I discovered her amazing work.

With the help of this new book, I did her meditation yesterday on how to find the colored thread that unites all the goodness, creativity, and help that we've given throughout our whole lives since we were little, up to now. We were supposed to reflect on all the good acts of kindness, of charity, caring, etc., that we've done for others in the world. I tried really hard with this exercise. I got settled, and still, and meditated on this prompt for about twenty minutes.

Usually, when I meditate, all this cool stuff pops up with her prompts—all these memories that I did this, or this was done for me, etc. But this particular one left me stumped. Nothing came up. Nada. I felt a huge feeling of emptiness swallow me whole, like a ragged gap in my existence. Nothing came up while I was racking my brain to find some inkling of good deeds, charity, helping, or CARING about others, or even myself. This exercise went deep; it took me to a very sad and lonely place, indeed!

So, maybe it wasn't the bagel I had for breakfast yesterday, instead of my usual oatmeal, that caused this to happen. I was thinking that maybe I'm gluten intolerant and I'd had a huge reaction to the wheat in the bagel. But this meditation was before breakfast. Or maybe it wasn't the ointment that I'd put in my eye. I read later that erythromycin, the antibiotic, could cause signs of depression or psychosis. Maybe it wasn't that either.

I didn't have the courage to dance. I didn't want to do the happy dance yesterday, or draw about it, or write about it. All I felt like doing was having a pity party on the sofa by myself, and be sad, and sulk, and maybe pick up my novel (a funny one, even), and try to finish the story with one blurry eye due to the ointment that I had to stick in it five times a day. My eye was red, itchy, painful, and blurry, and looked like—and still looks like—hell. And, of course, I forgot to stretch the bottoms of my feet upon waking, so I got up and felt that familiar 'rip' in my sole (hmmm, soul?) due to my recent bout with planter fasciitis. Crap.

So, that's another reason why I wanted to disappear and just be sad, lazy, lethargic, and hide myself from the world like our sixteen-year-old kitty who just lies on the stairs and snores most of the day, until dinner time. I think she pretends to be deaf, just so she can ignore us, and I wanted to do the same. I couldn't snap out of this terrible funk; it reminded me painfully of how I'd felt a few times in my life when I went into a real depression.

I'd been depressed due to a) injury (in college, when I had to leave the track team and learned I could never run again); b) a broken heart (a girlfriend broke up with me at my own birthday party in Brussels many, many years ago); c) losing a job or two, or knowing that I'd be fired eventually, which was out of my control. These signs and symptoms of deep sadness, depression, lethargy, and loneliness, but not wanting any company, not even my partner's, came back in full force yesterday and scared the heck out of me.

Now, I realize it was probably not the bagel, but it could've been the stye in my eye, my painful feet... and the cold, cloudy weather... but most likely it was two things: 1) going to the pharmacy the night before in a bandana, trying to cover my mouth and nose while I picked up my eye prescription, and feeling extreme fear about getting the coronavirus, and 2) sadness at seeing the empty place, and the lone worker at the counter, who spoke to me and took forever with the customer before me, who was six feet away, of course.

I think I got the employee's pain body and took it home with me. I felt a deep sadness about the situation and my realization that he and the pharmacist—a young Asian woman who gave me my ointment—were surely feeling scared, helpless, and all the rest right now during this health pandemic, putting their lives on the line to serve others. Being an empath, I'm pretty sure *that* is what made me feel deeply moved, sad, and scared for myself and all of humanity.

What I'd experienced last night was an extreme contrast to what I was feeling as I attempted to conjure up images and thoughts about how I'd served and cared for others from birth until now. And guess what? I couldn't find *any* trace of me caring for, or caring about, other people... until I was forty years old! Nothing, except caring for my two kitty cats... and I guess myself, somehow, but not really caring about me, either.

It was a shock, to say the least, to go back in time and realize how I'd never learned to care about others, put myself in their place, or do something to help them. I'm sure there must've been times when I did this, but I couldn't recall them yesterday. Instead, I sat on the sofa and didn't cry, but I sure did FEEL.

I realized my parents didn't care, either. Certainly not Dad. Mom tried to save the world, the oceans, the planet, even young, abused children outside our household, when I was growing up. It's strange that she didn't think to look inside our household. There was certainly a lot of stuff going on there. I guess closer to home was too painful. So, she put all her efforts outside and left us to our own forces. Self-preservation and survival were what I taught myself by watching her get by in this world. Maybe that's what Dad was doing, too. So, that's what I did until I was forty, before I started realizing that I needed to help others who had been wronged, not cared for, and not really loved in this world.

This realization yesterday hit me hard, like a baseball slammed into my gut, and my heart. I'm fifty-five. That's fifteen years of caring, loving, and trying to help humanity evolve. What the heck was wrong with me, during all those forty years of emptiness? I guess I was trying to keep my head above water. Trying to breathe. Trying to stay ALIVE.

So, for the next forty years of my life, until I'm ninety-five, I vow to do things differently. I guess it was a realization I needed to make, a terrible gray fog I needed to wade through, and now I'm on the other side—in less than twenty-four hours, luckily. I'll do the happy dance today, and I hope my days will become brighter from now on.

April 5th, 2020, Sunday, 3:20pm, Day 27 continued

I danced the 5Rhythms today in our online class, going in very frustrated and angry. The music to warm up went on, and I didn't know what was happening. Over Zoom, our teacher was dancing, warming up on the screen, and I thought she'd started the wave without us. I was frustrated, to say the least, and angry. When she said, "How are you all feeling? Make a movement to show us," I made two 'thumbs down.' It's amazing how angry I can get over dance, and technology, and being cooped up, and having last-minute surprises like that, which throw me off track. Maybe it's an ADHD thing.

So, finally, when she said, "*Now*, how are you feeling?" two seconds later, "Make another movement," I wanted to flash the birdie at the whole world. Luckily, I didn't. I'm no longer thirteen, right? Instead, I sat on my hand and gave a tired, lopsided smile to the webcam on my laptop. After thirty minutes of listening to everyone talk, and share, I was ready to explode. I really, really, just wanted to dance.

Finally, we were about to start, and then my partner dropped my computer. Fortunately, it didn't break, but we got kicked off the Zoom meeting. I was livid! And then it was time to take my eye medicine, and my partner forgot to wipe off the tube afterwards; she touched my eye, on top of that. It wasn't her fault, but I was already in a rotten mood.

Our dance session started out terrible, but I still danced. I did an angry *Staccato*, having missed the *Flowing* part of the music at the beginning of the wave. At the end, I did the happy dance, on my back, with my knees open, and my arms behind my head, swaying gently, opening up to the earth and sky, releasing, relaxing, and silently asking for forgiveness, by opening up and being vulnerable to what *is*, to what I felt in that sweaty moment, after dancing out my emotions and releasing my negativity.

I was able to cast out my frustrations like a heavy anchor, like I'd cut the chain. At one point, though, I felt the anchor pulling me down, leading me deeper and deeper into the ocean's depth. I lost my breath as I plunged. I can't stand heavy metal, and there was a song at the beginning of *Chaos*, the third rhythm, after *Flowing* and *Staccato*, and it was heavy metal, which grated on my body, ripping it to shreds, like someone furiously grating my flesh into soft cheese. At that point, when I made a face and whispered, "I hate this," my partner said, "Try to see why you hate it so much." She was right.

What is this hatred of this type of music—and this song, in particular, which enflames my nerves—teaching me about who I am as a person? What's the lesson? I'm trying to figure it out, *ouftie*, that's a term from the South of Belgium—in dialect—that only *Liègeois* people say (those from the city of Liège). I'm not *Liègeoise*, but it just came out as I'm writing this, for some reason. I'm not always sure why these things pop out, and then end up on the page.

Anyway, the heavy metal stopped, and a male voice came on, with instrumentals, and the sound became more *Lyrical*—softer, lighter, and more pleasant. Then the heavy metal came back, like poison darts, spiking the song with venom, and my nerves got all crispy, like dried up grass fried in oil. Why do I keep writing with metaphors?

After dancing the 5Rhythms we spoke for about fifteen minutes, and Maya, our teacher, said that this particular song, which was a mixture of *Chaos* and *Lyrical*, could really move people. Well, it sure moved me. She said we could listen to it again, and again, but frankly, once was enough for me, for now. She also said, "We're all in the same storm, but in different boats…and we have the freedom to f… it up!" I thought that was really true, and most of us nodded in agreement when she said it. Dancing sure gets us in tune with our emotions.

It's Sunday afternoon and it's the last day of spring break, I have tons of things to do, and I want to do ABSOLUTELY NOTHING right now. I want to lie on the sofa, like our cat, Sakura, whose back is facing me because she's angry. We put her favorite pillow out to air, and she can tell I'm still agitated about so many things right now, I'm hardly breathing. But I'm getting all this crap out of my system—at least, it seems like I am. There's been a backlog, a buildup of crap, that's been draining me of energy for years. It's high time to clean it out. Spring cleaning. Start resetting the program: control—alt—delete. RELAX.

April 6, 2020, Monday, Day 28

I'm feeling pressure again to perform, be the best, take care of all my students, be a perfectionist, do too much, and not take care of myself. I feel the squeeze of time on my shoulders and pressing against my temples. I woke up in the middle of the night with a splitting headache, scared it might be the virus, but sure it was the white wine. I never drink this stuff, even though it tastes okay. Now I remember *why*. I went for a wet, brisk walk with my partner under soggy rain clouds and bursts of sprinkles. We were all bundled up—it was cold out there—and we remained silent most of the way. I think we both prefer that right now. Silence. Being at one with nature, and with the 'now.'

My favorite part is when we reach our little park, even though we can't go in. Leading up to it is a pathway lined with trees and beautiful, dark, lush bushes, and the floor is made of cedar chips. It crunches when we walk, except today, when it sounded like soggy cereal under our sneakers. The air is fresh and cool, with yellow flowers growing out of the dark green bushes along the path.

When we're in there, I'm transported back to Kyoto, where there's a bamboo forest. It's quiet, peaceful, and luscious. I could stay there all day and soak up the positive energy from nature (negative ions), but I can't. Now, we must keep moving, showing we're exercising, and staying off the trails; otherwise, we could be fined $1,000 and/or spend six months in jail. They fined twenty-five people yesterday. I saw it on the news. We're not rich enough to afford that, so we keep trudging on, leaving the park as a glimpse of peaceful bliss each morning.

We used to sit there on our favorite bench in the sun, under the trees, and meditate. Until a dog would come licking at our knees or a kid would scream on the swing, waking us from our reverie. Now, it's all wet, damp, and eerily empty, with COVID-19 scaring everyone into their homes to stay, only venturing out for essentials.

My eye is a bit better today, but it still hurts and itches. I'm sort of afraid of skin cancer. I looked it up online today. I believe I have it and I believe our cat has it, too. We both have pain and redness in our left eyes, but there's nothing I can do but hope these antibiotics take the symptoms away. Feeling the stress, feeling the tension in our cozy condo, feeling that I'm pressured, with piles of things to file, taxes yet to finish, classes to be organized, than taught, grades to deliver, emails to read, and send, then delete—and the ones that I don't send, which stay in the drafts folder forever, because I can't decide about my life right now.

I don't want to commit to anything. Not one semester, not one year, not two years, not even tomorrow. I want to live right here, right now, and be present, blossom, and bloom—like my little seedlings that I'm carefully watering two to three times per day. It takes patience, love, care, compassion, and optimism to grow and blossom.

It's like writing a book; like this book. It's about dance, the happy dance, the slow dance, the *feeling* dance, and sometimes this dance makes me feel raw, like right now, like I was just cut into—like slicing an onion with a sharp knife. There's that splitting sound, the pungent sting, and sharp odor—the burst of taste on the tongue. It's a lot to take in, this rawness, this unsettling rawness, but I need to pass through it, like a dark tunnel, to get to the other side.

This too shall pass.

I stood in our small patio after my usual three to five-minute shake, standing in front of the Buddha statue, all wet and glistening outside—not me, I'm inside; the Buddha sits calmly in his usual spot next to the palm tree and the new garden planter, amongst our green, wet plants. I stood, silent, without moving. Just feeling, trying not to think. Just feeling the tips of my fingers and the ends of my toes, with my feet planted solidly on the ground. And I swayed a bit, and revolved a bit, like I was on a spring ready to spring/sprout/emerge from my frozen spot in the living room.

I'm tired of being inert; tired of being lazy, but at the same time, I just want to duck, hide, and go into a cocoon until this sticky, hot mess is over.

BURDEN

HEAVY LOAD
CONCERN FOR
OTHERS

EYE NOT
HEALED

Day 29

SADNESS STRIKES

WHEN
WILL
THIS
END?

PROBLEMS W/ ZOOM,
STUDENT VIDEOS,
PEOPLE NOT SHOWING-UP

SAD HEART

LOTS, LOTS OF RAIN
WET... WET CAT
LICKING
RAIN LETTUCE

TENSION AT
HOME!

← EARS RINGING (TINNITUS)

(GETTING THINNER—NO PROTEIN— BECAME
VEGETARIAN —NO MEAT, VERY
LITTLE CHEESE, MILK, ETC.) LOTS OF
SALAD, MILK, OATS — SOME FRUIT

(* HAS CORONA VIRUS)

FEET NOT WANTING TO
MOVE. PLANTED ON GROUND LIKE CEMENT
BLOCKS. FRIEND* DOESN'T ANSWER

Day 30

CLASS TODAY W/ JEAN + 14 OTHERS VIA ZOOM
COMPUTER ON A CHAIR

GALLERY VIEW

(GOOD TO BE
BACK IN CLASS)

ME UPSIDE DOWN

DOING THE SMALL
DANCE
WITH MY
SHOES ON
(PLANTAR
FASCIITIS)

WEIRD TO BE
HERE ALONE IN
MY LIVING ROOM

CARPET

CAT
WATCHING

STILL A   RAINY DAY
BIT OF SADNESS —   AGAIN

Day 31

clean hair → SPIRALING
ROTATING

FOOT IS BETTER, EYE
IS BETTER, BUT
ENEMA STARTED
ON RIGHT HAND.

FEELING GRAVITY
+ ROUNDNESS OF EARTH

← eye better

WHAT IS GOING ON IN
MY BODY?

WARMTH,
AFTER HOT
SHOWER +
WASHING HAIR

(HANGE IN DIET —
NOW VEGETARIAN.

LOST 5 LBS AT LEAST. WALKING,
DANCING, SLEEPING, WORKING ON
CLASSES FOR STUDENTS ONLINE.
+ LOTS OF WRITING + MEDITATING
+ TRYING TO HELP OTHERS. —

EARTH
ROUND
(ALONE
TIME W/
SOFT MUSIC)

EYE
BETTER

Day 32

TONS OF RAIN TODAY
NON-STOP +

HAPPY DANCE HAPPY
DAY!
Yeah! It's the
weekend!

ELECTRICAL OUTAGE
DURING MY ZOOM
CLASSES (OUCH! STRESS!

BRIGHTER MOOD

I HAVE TO GRADE,
TONS, BUT NO MORE
CLASSES EXCEPT
DANCE // 5 RHYTHMS.

ATE CARROT
TOPS IN
MY KALE
SALAD TODAY. GREW
THEM MYSELF IN A
TRAY !!!

MY AUNT ISN'T
SICK WITH COVID-19
AFTER ALL!

FOOT
BETTER

WATER
EVERYWHERE

FLOODING!
SO MUCH RAIN

SLEEPING REALLY WELL + lost 5 Lbs!

Sketchbook, Days 29 to 32

April 7th, 2020, Tuesday, Day 29

I'm not feeling happy at all, so the happy dance wasn't a fun thing, but it did move me inside, even though I hardly moved outside with my feet and body. I feel like I want to cry all the time. There's a lot of tension here at home between my partner and me. We're cooped up in a small space and there's nowhere to go. She likes her loud music and funny videos; I like silence and stillness, and I'm not in the mood to laugh.

We try to share the space as best as possible, but today I came downstairs at 5:00am because I couldn't sleep. That's my time to be alone, to write, meditate, and read inspirational, deep, thought-provoking books. She came down and wanted me to watch a funny video that her friend sent her, but I didn't want to. That was my sacred space on the couch, with our cat. I just wanted to curl up and be alone in silence, so she went back upstairs to bed. Sad, isn't it?

These kinds of things are common lately, now that neither of us can go outside, except to exercise. I tried for three hours yesterday to get a delivery of food from a well-known online shopping site and a local grocery store, to no avail. My eyes, which already sting, were stinging even more after that. It's a sad time; a time of grief, anxiety, pain, and… hope, as well.

I hope people get over this virus. I hope this ends soon. I hope people treat each other better after this crisis. I hope they become less self-centered and greedy, and more compassionate, caring, and generous with others. And I hope they learn their lesson: that we all need to respect this planet, all living beings, and our natural resources. Otherwise, we're doomed.

My entire Ph.D. dissertation was on this very subject, so it touches me deeply. I spent six years researching our connection to nature in northern Japan, where the earthquake and tsunami hit on March 11th, 2011, killing so many people—even some of my close friends—and ruining their livelihoods, agriculture, and beautiful landscape.

I'm still so sad about what happened in Sendai and Fukushima. My friends were cooped up for at least six months afterwards and couldn't even open a window because of the radiation. This pandemic reminds me of that, what they all went through. The world is going through this terrible transition now, all over the planet. It's scary, it really is. I'm sad. And I have tons of work to do for school. Pressures, papers, reports, presentations, slides, emails—it all piles up—*MERDE, quoi.*

On top of this, I've lost some weight—probably muscle mass, but also because we haven't been eating much protein. We can't seem to order any, and we don't want to go to the store for fear of contamination. So, we'll just keep eating vegetables. At least we have those. I hope today gets better. It's rainy, cold, and gloomy. I'll try to stay optimistic, but one of my good friends in Belgium has the virus, and I still haven't heard back from her. It's been a week. ☹

April 8th, 2020, Wednesday, Day 30

We had our online dance class today with Jean and I took some notes, but they're upstairs and it's nearly 9:00pm and I'm feeling lazy. I'll write about our class tomorrow, after my happy dance, which I learned (relearned?) today is supposed to be called the 'small dance.' But I'm not the only one who confuses this term. Another student said, 'slow dance,' and another called it the 'big dance.' So, I don't feel so bad. Happy dance is the best term, though, even when you're sad, like I was yesterday, and a couple of days ago. We each spoke in turn via Zoom, and I shared how my life was a rollercoaster lately, and how I was too sad to do the happy dance, or even write in my journal one day. I'll write more tomorrow. I'm exhausted after seven hours of Zoom today...

April 9th, 2020, Thursday, Day 31

I'm sitting on another part of the couch now. My partner hates our living room table, so we agreed to move it into the hallway to give us more room to dance and do yoga. It *is* nice to have more space. But now, without the table, I can't see my books or find a place to put my tea set, and I drink tea when I meditate, write, and read. So, it wasn't so great when I spilled the tea just now after my happy dance, because I tried to put my teacup on the little side table next to me on the sofa. Not a great move.

I can't see the Buddha statue from here, but I can see the front door, so in Japan, at least, I'm in the place of honor, like a samurai. And I see our potato tree, with all its beautiful decorations, including the one I added a few weeks ago that says PEACE on it. I hung it on the tree after stashing it in the garage for six years. I'd painted the words on a slab of wood when I had less work and some extra paint and glitter. I should make more things like that and give them away as offerings to our friends, family, and neighbors, especially during this difficult time, when we're all homebound.

We're running out of oatmeal, which I eat every morning. And we're running out of plenty of other things, like protein. So why did I all of a sudden develop eczema on my right hand, over the four knuckles? What am I doing wrong? My diet is much better (vegetarian), although I don't really have protein right now, except for a little dried salmon in our soup. I stopped the eye antibiotic because it was killing me, with all the itching, redness, pain, and blurry vision. My eye is much better now. But I do wash my hands about a hundred times per day, and maybe that's what caused the eczema. I put on some heavy-duty cream before going to bed, and that helped a bit, but it's still rough, scaly, itchy, and painful over the knuckles.

I also went for a brisk walk between rain showers this morning, and found a nice flower pot I needed to plant my carrot tops in. It was in the recycling bin at a neighbor's and perfect—exactly what I'd decided I needed this morning—and PAF! There it was, sticking out of the bin on my walk! Couldn't have found a better one. I thought of the biblical verse, "Ask and you shall receive." I think it's biblical, anyway, but I have no idea where it is in the Bible, of course. So, I'll keep asking, and I hope I can keep receiving.

I'm going to go work a bit upstairs before my webinar via Zoom at noon. I had three Zoom classes yesterday to teach, in addition to Jean's dance class, and my 5Rhythms Heartbeat™ test class last night via Zoom, where we danced for nearly an hour, and tested the music for our instructor to use on Sundays. It was cool. Two of the dancers were in Mexico.

This pandemic is super scary, but it's at least uniting people, via the Internet, all over the world. And boy does Mother Nature seem to love the rain, and the sudden drop in pollution levels, all over the globe. Also, so many people, like me, are slowing down enough to finally appreciate nature's gifts to the universe, to us, and everyone around us.

Unfortunately, some people are taking advantage of this situation, like this scammer/spammer/phisher who just called my cell phone. And others, so many others, are suffering, like my partner, because they've lost their employment. It will all work out though, I'm sure it will. I have to keep doing the happy dance—no matter what.

April 10th, 2020, Friday, Day 32

It's 5:45pm and I'm exhausted, of course. I had a two-hour faculty learning community Zoom meeting, and I presented some material on mindfulness in the classroom. It went well, then I gave two classes via Zoom, and our electricity went out! Luckily, it was at the end of one class, at 1:25, and the blackout went until 1:35pm, so I only started five minutes late. I thought I'd been Zoom bombed. The screen went white and my wi-fi went straight to another person's. I didn't know whose it was. Really scary. But now the electricity and wi-fi are back on, and all went well with my class.

It hasn't stopped raining since yesterday and there's flooding everywhere, including inside our garage. I haven't been out, but I did dust and vacuum our bedroom, which serves as my office. My partner asked what all the noise was; she was beaming when she saw what I was doing. It's not my favorite sport, so it takes me longer to get motivated. Cleaning our bedroom was on my list to do for several days.

Now, finally, I did my happy dance in the living room. We moved the living room table into the doorway area, and now we can dance, do yoga, and lie down on the floor all day. It's like our own miniscule private yoga studio/dance studio.

In fact, we did gentle yoga about an hour ago, side by side, and that was really cool. From our living room, we could watch the rain outside, the plants, our Buddha, the trees, etc., and nobody could see us. Lovely adaptation, I'd say. The happy dance today was really grounding. I only did about five minutes of warm-up, shaking and moving, and about five minutes of the silent, happy (small) dance. I felt really centered and calm and could concentrate a lot while standing and swaying. I noticed that I was touching my knees as I was doing it, and I wondered why. It doesn't matter why. I was simply doing what my knees felt like doing at that moment in time. I didn't feel dizzy at all.

Now, however, my partner has decided to dance in this small space in front of me, and she's doing the airplane, pirouettes, jerking motions, and tapping her chest like a lion to the music of Milène Farmer, a French singer who I really like. My partner wants my attention and it makes her laugh that I'm trying to write diligently in my dance journal—trying to concentrate, as usual—while she's dancing in front of me. This is very funny, and fun. I think I'll stop writing because she's dancing up a storm—even on the furniture next to me. I give up because I want to dance with her, too.

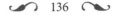

HAPPY DANCING IN KITCHEN! PARTLY CLOUDY **Day 33** LIKE A VACATION Sunny, too!

SUNSHINE IN KITCHEN WINDOW

too SHORT

COOKING SOUP

(CARROT TOPS + LEEK TOPS + 1 POTATO)

MAKING PESTO W/ RADISH TOPS

OH WELL!

MUSIC (MUSIQUE FRANÇAISE)

(SPONTANEOUS BURSTS OF DANCE!!)

NOT WORKING OR GRADING IN MORNING

ITS SATURDAY! PLANTING CARROTS + OTHER VEGGIES + COOKING

WORRIED:

Day 34 EASTER SUNDAY CLOUDY SKIES

AND THE NEIGHBORS WILL LIKE? MOM

5 RHYTHMS DANCING W/ MY PARTNER + OUR TRIBE VIA ZOOM

BOOM BOOM BOOM

FUN TO DO IT TOGETHER

MUSIC (LOUD)

STACCATO + CHAOS

VIA STEREO SPEAKERS!

JOYFUL HAPPY UNLEASHED

& THEN HAPPY DANCE IN STILLNESS

TUNING IN

SHARING W/ TRIBE

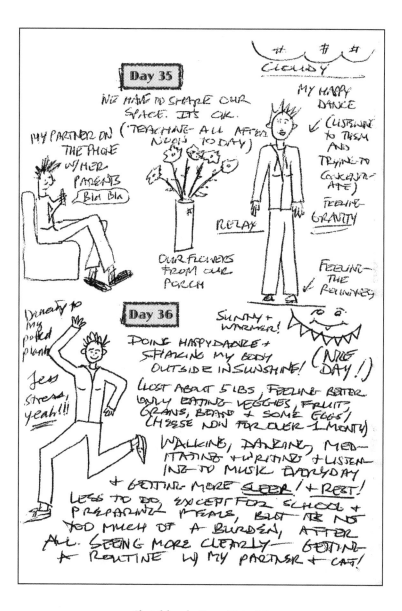

Sketchbook, Days 33 to 36

April 11th, 2020, Saturday, Day 33

Today, I got up late, at 9:15am, and I was going to work and post stuff and grade papers, etc., but I didn't feel like it. So, I had breakfast with my partner and didn't even meditate, or write in my journal, do yoga, or even stretch. We went outside to walk because it was sunny for the first time in a week, and then I decided to plant the carrot tops that I've been growing for ten days in the kitchen. They've been soaking in a watery pan next to the sink. I wanted to make a soup out of other carrot tops, now that I've found out they aren't poisonous, and leek tops. So I did. And I made pesto out of radish tops—not poisonous either and quite edible, but peppery. By then, it was 3:30pm, and I did some work until 5:00pm.

Then we went for a drive because my car battery will die if I don't use the car and it's been ten days. We walked near the beach—about six streets away from it, actually—but we could still see crashing waves and smell the ocean. I desperately wanted to go into all the stores, even a fast-food restaurant, which I don't ever, ever eat, since I was partially raised on that crap, but I wanted to go in and eat everything in sight, and buy toilet paper because we can't get it anywhere. What a discovery: I miss shopping, of all things.

As I was cooking in the kitchen, it occurred to me to open the window extra wide, to let in the sunshine, and play music. So, I put on some French music and danced. It was great! I really liked moving around in the small, rectangular space at the center of our kitchen, with its cool, tile floor. I was in my shoes because of my planter fasciitis, unfortunately, but I still danced, moving my hips, shoulders, head, etc.

My partner thought it was a bit silly to dance there, especially since people walking by could see me through the window, but nobody was, so nobody did. Besides, it's *our* kitchen, so we can do what we want in it, right? It felt liberating and right to dance at that very moment instead of working on my computer.

It's Saturday, and tomorrow is Easter Sunday; even though I'm not a Christian anymore, I can still appreciate holidays for others. Now, I'm hearing the bread maker make rice bread—the only flour I could get through a major online shopping site; it's supposedly intended to make noodles—and I can hear French music in the background, and my partner drying her hair with our VERY LOUD blow dryer. I'm so sensitive to noise, it's insane.

Well, I'll go back to my happy dance tomorrow. I'll do it before 5Rhythms, I suppose. But, then again, it's the weekend, so who knows what will happen? Liberty, freedom, resistance to the *status quoi*—what? I meant to write status quo. That's all this shelter-in-place is bringing out of me!!! How weird is that? *Status quoi? Quoi* in French means "what"!

April 12th, 2020, Sunday, Day 34

Today, I was able to do my happy dance after dancing with our 5Rhythms group and my partner via Zoom. It's the fifth week in a row that we've done this, and it was really cool. I worried about our neighbors knocking on our door, asking us if we were having a party for Easter, because we NEVER make noise and there we were, with our stereo system playing loud music, and me wearing my earplugs. I wondered if they thought we'd gone mad, or if they were wringing their hands and shaking their heads.

I also thought about the person who shot six people yesterday in Bakersfield, because they had organized a social gathering in their home, and our neighbor hates us, and has personally threatened me, saying I'm a "terrible person," for no reason. It could be because he doesn't respect us, because we're two women living together—and not like 'roommates,' as he must've thought when we moved in seven years ago. So, I was a bit concerned for our safety, but after the wave, which lasted forty-two minutes, we ended in *Stillness*. That's when I did the happy dance, and all was well. We were still alive and very much here.

I also worried that my mom would call during this time because it's Easter Sunday, and both my brothers called already this morning, but not my mom. Luckily, she forgot about us, or else she was busy Zooming in with her church. Our church, for my partner and me, is dancing on Sundays, dancing the 5Rhythms, feeling, moving, meditating, and being in *Stillness* afterwards. "Sweating our prayers," as Gabrielle Roth, the founder of 5Rhythms, would say, like she did in one of the books she wrote, "Sweat Your Prayers," which I readily devoured.

This morning, I read one of the three articles that Jean gave us to study before class on Wednesday because I got up early, at 6:30am. It was about contact improvisation, identity, oppression, etc. I'll probably read it again before Wednesday's class. And there's

Laura Kline

a one-hour video that I'll watch maybe tonight, too.

It's a time to slow down, look inside, and really appreciate the present moment. I have *tons* of work to do for school, even though I only have three classes this semester, because we're doing remote learning now. Well, my partner says I'm doing too much, I'm not even paid for this extra work, and it's killing the battery in my computer. I'm not getting a new one either. Maybe she's right. But I can't just leave my students to fend for themselves, can I? I have a conscience. Well, I'm going to make lunch now. Not a proper Easter Sunday lunch, just a veggie soup with beans that I made yesterday, and kale salad with tuna, perhaps. We're trying to stay healthy and fit... We'll see!

April 14th, 2020, Tuesday, Day 36

Yesterday I didn't write in here, I had so much to do with my three Zoom classes and online office hours. At 5:15pm, when I finished, we went for a much-needed walk in the foggy, cool afternoon, and I was beat. All I wanted to do was lie down on the sofa and relax, or read, or do both. I did manage to dance and 'shake it out' for about five minutes, then do my happy dance of relative stillness—to gain mindful awareness of my internal state and my external relationship to my surroundings—before collapsing. I didn't feel like expending any more energy writing in this journal (I also write in my regular, daily journal each morning in French), so that's a lot when you add all the energy it takes to teach three classes, etc., during the day.

I decided to simply do a drawing of what I did, and how I felt yesterday. For Day 35, I drew my partner on the phone, talking to her parents in Belgium, because it was Easter Monday, and it's a holiday there on Monday, not like here, on Sunday. And I was looking at the flowers I'd picked from our front porch area. The gardener usually cuts them but because the home association for our condos has told the gardeners not to come, I got to cut them instead these past two weeks! I was trying to do my happy dance and not listen to too much of her conversation, but I did still listen, and then I drew, and plopped on the sofa to relax, finally.

Today was different. I have wet hair because I took a shower to get off all the grime after walking with my partner on our morning's walk, up and down this big hill near here. Then I decided to dance in our little patio because it's finally sunny and a bit warmer (68 degrees Fahrenheit) outside, and I figured it would dry my hair. Who cares about the neighbors seeing me dance through the fence? I don't care at this point.

I also unveiled our little planter that we put together, letting the tiny sprouts experience the fresh warm air as well. I watched them as I danced in the sun, and heard the rustling leaves from the palm tree, and the birds chirping overhead. It was really, really cool.

Unfortunately, I found a mole on my upper left thigh last night before going to bed, which I hadn't noticed before. It was a bit scratchy and brown colored, and the sides weren't very regular. It looked grayish inside, so all of this kind of scared me.

This morning, I checked, and it was still there. I measured it against a pencil eraser and it's a bit smaller. I took a photo of it with my camera, because I can zoom in and inspect it. It was broken up, with little yellowish clumps. Not very nice looking at all.

What's weird was I was looking at a skin cancer website last week because someone I know has had basal cell and squamous cell carcinoma, even though she says she's never had skin cancer. I disagreed, so I was looking it up to prove I was right, and there were all these pictures of what skin cancer looked like. Of course, I saw images of things that I have on my arms, legs, back, etc., myself. But not this particular one. So, it was kind of scary, and I wondered if my dermatologist knew what she was doing. And then, PAF! Last night, I find this little mole on my leg. That woman's first skin cancer was on her leg, too.

Oh well, I'll just monitor it, and we'll see what happens. My partner says that maybe it's my body's way of getting rid of toxins. Maybe. That would be cool. But I spend lots more time outdoors walking around than I did before… even though I always wear a hat, and sunscreen, and the tops of my thighs never see the sun! Despite this, I'll do the happy dance outside again tomorrow if it's sunny, even without wet hair!

We danced today w/ Jean via Zoom. Sunny weather again. Hot (inside, though, it's cold).

Day 37

HMM

I'm outside but the neighbor is busying, boring + grinding with his machines again. I hate that!! NOISY!

DOING CONTACT IMPROVE AROUND SAKURA, AND WITH HER. SHE'LL PROBABLY JOIN US EACH TIME, NOW!

← STRETCH →

SOFT, SLEEK FUR, WARM, CAT-LIKE SMELL

PURR PURR

↙ SAKURA, OUR CAT, ON MY YOGA MAT

SHE'S SO HAPPY TO JOIN US (ME TOO!)

INTERESTING, FUN EXPERIENCE!

Day 38

SUNNY

TRYING TO IGNORE THE LOUD NEIGHBOR YELLING AT HER KIDS.

AND THE CAR ALARM THAT WON'T STOP GOING OFF.

AND MY DELIVERY OF AN EMPTY ENVELOPE!

DANCING OUT IN PATIO!

IN FRONT OF MY LITTLE PLANTS — WATCHING THEM GROW!

TRYING TO IGNORE ALL THAT AND JUST BE IN THE MOMENT. FEELS GOOD TO MOVE/DANCE.

EVERY DAY BLENDS INTO NEXT DAY

Day 39

CLOUDY W/ A BIT OF A SHY SUN TODAY

AM I REALLY LAZY?

HAIR GROWING - NOT CUTTING! WEARING MASK + SUNGLASSES FOR PROTECTION

(GOT GOOD EVALUATION AT SCHOOL - A BIT RELIEVED)

STILL NEED TO DO TAXES!

DANCING IN PATIO!

FIXED KINK IN BACK TOO! (TIRED, TOO!)

SO MUCH WORK TO DO BUT ALL I WANT TO DO IS RELAX + PLAY!

GOT UP REALLY EARLY (THINKING ABOUT EVALS) AND MADE SOUP FOR MOM.

Day 40

PROCRASTINATE LEAD TO!

SUNNY BUT COOL

FEELING GOOD, OVERALL

WORK, WORK, WORK!

ALL DAY SATURDAY! NEED TO GET COURSES READY FOR MONDAY. ALL I WANT TO DO IS RELAX, WALK, PLAY + HAVE A PARTY!!

DID SOME YOGA

ARCHED BACK

AND WALKED 3X (TAKING PICTURES W/ PARTNER OF FLOWERS + TREES)

Camera CLICK!

+ GARDENED A BIT (PLANTED CARROTS)

Sketchbook, Days 37 to 40

April 15th, 2020, Wednesday (partially written during Jean's class), Day 37

"What if the world meets our dancing?" That's what Jean asked us. It was a good dancing session today and Sakura, my cat, decided to lay on my yoga mat in the middle of my living room. So, I danced around her, using Jean's prompts. We had touch and contact improvisation, and I was also worried about my computer running out of juice. I started the Zoom session at 65%, and now the battery is at 19%, so I wonder if it will last (we have twenty-five more minutes left in this class).

Some of us cried when one of the students said, "Thank you," to Jean for caring so much, and for showing up for her students. I got teary, myself. Jean did, for sure, and I bet Susie did, too. It's hard to read everyone's emotions through the computer screen. We had a choice to just reflect, or to write, for this last part of class, and of course, I chose to write, which I'm doing now.

We're going to share what Nancy Stark Smith calls "harvesting," for sharing, "titrate," "modulate," or change the response to stimulus, etc., with the discomfort of being seen, in person or on screen, via video. I kept checking to see if I was doing it right. These are some of the things we talked about: "Hide self,"— you won't see yourself— interesting view in Zoom. But they will see you. "What if these are the perfect conditions to learn what we need to learn?" (Jean's example). Ability to flip the perspective to see if there's something we need to learn from the situation. Watch ten-minute video for next week. Instagram: "The people I love" (Tina's comment). Reminders, too.

Now, class is over. Those were some brief notes that I wrote in here during class. They make sense to me now, but I doubt they will later. I stayed on the call for a few minutes today, to thank Jean and

Susie. There were three other students still on as well. I explained how great it was to have students feeling comfortable enough to show their faces on the screen in our class, because in my three Zoom classes that I'm teaching, only one student ever dares to show his face. All the others have their cameras off, so I feel really vulnerable and disconnected from my students, for the most part. Not like in this class at all.

I'm outside trying to relax as I write and appreciate nature, even though this idiot neighbor is always buzzing and cutting something metallic in his garage. The noise ruins all the peace and calmness out here, and he's like ten houses away, but it's really rude, disrespectful, and disturbing.

I also told Jean and Susie that this class was the best part of my week, and it's true. It's been like this since the beginning of the semester. Susie announced that students can already start enrolling in dance classes for the Fall. I really hope they get enough students! Now, I'll draw in my dance sketchbook. I showed both of these, my journal and sketchbook, to Jean, Susie, and the remaining three students on Zoom after class. They all clapped when they saw them.

Tomorrow's another day. So, I'll just live today then. Susie asked us, "What is the portal out?" and I wonder what it is. Dance?

April 16th, 2020, Thursday, Day 38

Imagine my frustration right now. Excited to get a package, I open an envelope from a major online shopping site, and there's nothing in it. It's absolutely empty! Really maddening. I'm not sure what object I ordered was supposed to be delivered, but I think it was a cleaning supply bottle. And perhaps the delivery person wanted it, and opened it, because these sealed plastic envelopes don't just open on their own. What do I do now? I have the empty envelope, so I took a picture of it. It makes me not want to do online shopping ever again.

This was right after I did a brief dance outside, then a five-minute happy dance in silence. I heard our neighbor who's always yelling at her kids scolding one of them, and saying that the boys would be back at 9:00am tomorrow. Shit. They're so loud! Then a car alarm went off in the parking lot (it's been happening a lot lately). Next, the delivery came with my empty package, and my partner's now on the phone, and really loud upstairs, so I just put on some soothing music to try to calm down.

I can't be outside because of the neighbor's grating voice on my system, the car alarm, and… well, I'm not sure what's worse. Sound is a really big part of my existence, and I'm super sensitive to it. The dancing part went well, though, and I was able to move, stretch, and do whatever I wanted. I don't care if the neighbors hear me or watch me. I really don't care. I danced for the plants in our patio, and even moved one, Gloria, to the top of our rain barrel because the barrel broke during a rainstorm on Friday and I don't want any dangerous mosquito-infecting things going inside to harm others or us.

Last night was really frustrating because we cancelled our Zoom happy hour with our friends for an impromptu dance class with our 5Rhythms dance teacher and we weren't able to enter the session. She accidentally locked it—or maybe it locked itself—at 6:04pm and we were trying to connect with my partner's computer for the first time. It was super frustrating because I was looking forward to dancing in our living room to great music with my partner and the other dancers.

Instead, we danced a bit our own, then we ate dinner, and had some wine, because we missed our happy hour after all. I was sad, and I know I shouldn't let disappointment at sudden changes of events sadden me, but maybe because I'd seen everyone in the morning, and danced with them, it really made me sad. I'd like to give big hugs to my friends, family members, colleagues, and even some students. Instead, I hug my partner a lot, and our kitty cat. And I take excellent care of our plants that I'm growing for food, etc.

We're supposed to get a food delivery this morning from a local grocery store. I was finally able to arrange one after a full month of trying! And it's not here yet. We'll see if it comes. I was supposed to get one last night for oatmeal from a local distributor and it never came. Oh well. This is all such an uncertain time for everyone. It's hard to stay sane sometimes. I create a routine, and the routine is broken, then I start a new routine, which is interrupted by another unexpected circumstance. Well, at least I'm practicing impermanence, patience, and resilience. Dance is teaching me this. It's grounding me and—I hope—making me stronger.

April 17th, 2020, Friday, Day 39

Today is the day they projected the peak in COVID-19 cases in California. We'll see. I keep up on the news three times a day, and that takes a lot of time. It took me a half day or more yesterday just to order and organize my grocery deliveries. We finally figured out how to do this online. Lots of stuff, like milk, cheese, yogurt, protein/meat, and toilet paper/paper towels are still missing. It reminds me of what my dad said about sugar and milk missing during the Great Depression, or was it World War II?

Anyway, I'm doing okay despite all these changes with the global pandemic. I feel like each day is blending into the next, however. It's a bit surreal. I never feel like I'm accomplishing much. I'm just getting by, and doing the minimum I need to do to slide by. I've never been like this before. I've always been a huge overachiever. Yep. Always— to the detriment of my health, sanity, career, relationships, and my general well-being. And now I'm slowing down so much that I'm actually nurturing myself for the first time ever. I could do so much more, though, like footbaths, naps, hot cocoa in the afternoons, reading for pleasure instead of studying, etc., but I don't.

I realize I'm gradually sliding into a self-preservation mode of quasi hibernation. I want to do all these cool art projects I've planned to do for years. I want to finish writing that novel that I started two years ago. I want to connect with my friends and see how they're doing. But instead, I'm becoming a lazy slob!

April 17th, 2020, Friday, Day 39 (continuation of last entry in first dance journal)

So much has happened this semester, I can't believe it. When I started this contact improvisation class in late January, I never knew that my last day on campus would be Friday, March 13th, less than two months later. I never imagined we'd have online dance classes with Zoom and we'd all be stuck in our homes for weeks and months, and only able to go out for exercise and essentials with masks and gloves on.

I never would've imagined a pandemic that would hit the entire world with such force, killing thousands, if not millions of people, making already twenty-two million Americans unemployed in the first month of its appearance in our country. I never would've imagined the stress, heartache, fear, and surge of rapid changes we're all experiencing, especially those on the front line: health care workers, grocery store workers, farmers, mail people, delivery people, pharmacists, etc., and the total collapse of the world economy, with no transportation by air, or car (barely), and so much more—tourism, stock markets, businesses small and large, restaurants, coffee shops, grocery stores, service industries—the works—up in smoke.

I didn't know what 'shelter-in-place order' meant until I experienced it first-hand over a month ago. This dance journal has evolved into much more than a dance journal. I'm doing my happy dance (small dance) religiously every day (except one day, when I was really depressed), and documenting what I do and how I feel directly afterwards with my pot of tea on the sofa. We took the living room table away to store our 'coronavirus' infected items, like food and mail, that have been delivered three days or less to our home. And we made room for us both to dance. Hence, the teapot on the sofa. It's kind of bohemian; I have to be careful not to spill my tea.

"I'm becoming a lazy slob" is my last sentence in dance journal number one, and I think I'll elaborate more on that sentence tomorrow. Now, I have to make tuna salad sandwiches and pack up the soup—made of kale tops, broccoli bottoms, one potato, a third of an onion, a few spices, and no broth, because we don't have any— that I made this morning for my mom. We're going to visit her at her home, but not go inside. We'll eat outside (six feet at least between us because we don't share the same household), and then we'll take a walk around her neighborhood and pick some of her oranges (we only have one left), and then go home. We're supposed to dance tonight, and we'll see how that goes!

April 18th, 2020, Saturday, Day 40

Today, I walked three times, took pictures, did some gardening, and yoga with my partner, then I worked most of the day on my courses. We'll dance tomorrow with 5Rhythms on Zoom, and that's always good. We did a free, experimental sound healing and dance class yesterday with a teacher whom we met via a friend and it was really bizarre. We had to say sounds like "Ah, Oh, Yeah!" etc., and do these strange rhythmic movements.

I wanted to laugh; it was so weird. Sticking out our tongues, feeling our sacrums, etc., then talking about how we felt. We were invited to this class, where thirteen women were paying this teacher, who was teaching from some sort of outdoor tent. The women were participating from all over the world. It was a bit ridiculous, and hilarious, and after sixty minutes, my partner and I politely excused ourselves. She was sweet to invite us into her group, but after that, we were more than ready for a happy hour to start our weekend.

During the night, I got really dizzy and kept thinking about Zoom meetings, and timing, which was all skewed. I woke up really thirsty—so did my partner—with a terrible stomachache and nausea. I was sick, and I wondered if it was caused by the sound healing, and the chanting, which I realized were Native American Indian chants, even though our teacher was blond, with long hair, a yoga-thin body, and looked just like a famous woman I've read about who tells people's astrology with homemade tarot cards. The dance teacher is not a Native American Indian, so I was wondering the whole time we were dancing about cultural appropriation and the ethics of her sacred-ish? seance.

I should've been more worried about its aftereffects, however, because I had a rather strong physical reaction in my intestines. Luckily, now, it's gone. Maybe the whole thing was healing, or

Laura Kline

perhaps it was that soup I made for dinner out of broccoli bottoms and kale tops. I didn't skin the broccoli stems, so the sharp points got stuck in our throats. Oh well! Time to do some more grading… Saturday night. *It's live!*

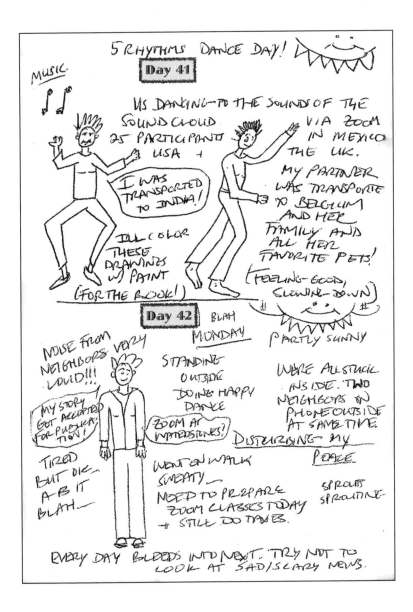

DAILY ROUTINE. WHEN WILL IT END?
???
UNKNOWN!
SUNNY

Day 43

SITTING WITH MY TEA, DRAWING + WRITING
IN MY DANCE JOURNAL. ALL IS PEACEFUL
(EXCEPT THE NOISY NEIGHBORS + MY PARTNER ON
THE PHONE WITH HER PARENTS)

WARM TEA

I LIKE TO DANCE OUT MY
KINKS IN THE BODY, THEN
STAND IN STILLNESS, FEEL-
ING THE
PEACE +
FULLNESS OF
THE MOMENT
WASHING OVER
(+ THROUGH)
MY BODY.
EVERY DAY.

I LIKE
SKETCHING
+
WRITING
IN MY
DANCE
JOURNAL

SECOND POT
TODAY!

SAKURASNORING!
ZZZ

Day 44

YIKES!

I CAN'T STAND THE NOISE ANY MORE!!! THE
NEIGHBOR HAS HIS MACHINE ON AND I DON'T KNOW
WHAT IT IS, BUT IT'S THE LOUDEST THING I'VE EVER
HEARD IN MY LIFE! I'M SITTING HERE TRYING
TO LISTEN TO A LETTER READ BY ASHTON T. CRAWLEY
LIVE INSTEAD OF OUR USUAL DANCE CLASS. EAR-
PHONES IN, SIPPING TEA, STRAINING TO HEAR
THROUGH THE TERRIBLE MACHINE NOISE THAT IS
SHAKING OUR WALLS AND FRAYING MY NERVES. ONLY
1 PERSON CLAPPED. I WAS PLANNING TO
DANCE TODAY W/ MY CLASS. INSTEAD I'M
SITTING HERE, SWEATING, AND — "THE LONELY
LETTERS" READING THE LIVESTREAM FEEDBACK.
LOTS OF HEARTS ON THE SCREEN. YEAH, HE STOPPED
THE HORRIBLE, SHAKING NOISE!
(W/MAYFIELD!)
NOISE!
NOISE! MACHINE!

FRUSTRATION!
AARGH!

EARBUDS
TRYING TO
LISTEN TO OUR CLASS' LIVESTREAM

Sketchbook, Days 41 to 44

April 19th, 2020, Sunday, Day 41

Today we danced with our 5Rhythms group via Zoom in our living room. The music wasn't too loud, so I was able to dance without my earplugs, and without worrying that the neighbors would have a heart attack, like I did last week. Not the heart attack, of course. Just worrying about it.

It was cool because our teacher, Maya, asked us to imagine that we were traveling to somewhere where we'd really like to go during our dance wave. I thought I'd go to India, because I've never been there, and one of the artists that she invited to our class is in India for the moment. Thirty percent of her songs came from there, I think. While dancing, I really felt like I was in India, with the vivid images, sensations, feelings, bright colors, and warmth. It was cool.

After that, I was just dancing and listening to the softness and *Stillness* of the music after *Chaos*, and suddenly, I saw all my drawings in my sketchbook for this class, and this dance journal. I imagined myself coloring each drawing, which I've done in black and white, with either coloring pencils or a watercolor brush. It looked really cool in my head and I imagined each drawing as the start of each journal entry, which will be a small chapter in my book about discovering dance, my happy dance, and especially myself during this coronavirus pandemic.

We went for a walk after lunch and I took lots of flower pictures and tree pictures, as usual. I watered my tiny sprouts in my little pots twice today already, and I thought about calling my brother and aunt later on today. Yesterday, I worked really hard to finish all that I needed to do for my classes, and I have a bit more to do today, so I'll be ready for my Zoom sessions tomorrow. I still wonder where some of my students are and how they're doing. They're not all answering my emails; about one-tenth are responding when I reach out to them to see how they're doing. If they drop off the grid, and about twenty percent are in this category, I'm getting no news from them, and very little responsiveness online. It's disconcerting.

Only three more weeks of online classes, then we'll have the online final exam. I'll be so ready for this semester to end. At the same time, I'm enjoying reading my students' online forum posts, and their papers about their use of information and communication technology, especially now, while they're at home and have little to do except schoolwork. It was fascinating to see how so many of them really did the assignment, and they did it well. I'm sure we would've had very different reactions in normal times, when everyone still had a normal lifestyle, with all its business and frenzy, and in-person classes.

I'd hoped to lose weight, but now that we got a few deliveries of new foods, that might not happen after all. Until tomorrow!

April 20ᵗʰ, 2020, Monday, Day 42

I have three Zoom remote class sessions to teach, record, and edit today, and my office hours. I want to get it over with because it's quite stressful and I won't have time to eat properly. I'll wash my hair first, because I record myself on the screen in a small window, in addition to my slides. I might cut the sides, too, because they're becoming bushy. The sides; not slides. ☺

I've been hungrier lately, so I ate at 11:00pm last night (a snack of yogurt with a bit of granola). Luckily, we got a delivery on Thursday, and when I weighed myself this morning, I weighed 600 grams more than yesterday. That might've been the timing, though. I did it right after a big breakfast of oatmeal, half a banana, and three types of fresh berries—thanks to the delivery again—and nuts and chia seeds. This is what I usually eat for breakfast (lots of fiber), with my tea and milk, after writing in my regular journal, in French.

This morning I'm super happy because one of my stories that I submitted like a year ago got accepted to an anthology, and I'll be working with editors to get it ready for publication. They said they "Loved it!" which makes me more confident as a creative writer/ memoirist. I'll also say "yes" to that bookstore in the UK to do some Zoom sessions. I don't like being on the screen, virtually, but since they had to cancel our annual book festival, I'd better do it.

And there's a book proposal review that I said "yes" to for an academic publisher, also in the UK. I'll only get sixty British Pounds, which is peanuts, but it's good for my CV (academic resume), and my current lack of income.

All day long, every day, I just sort of exist. I plan out my day's list of things to do each morning, before I do anything else, except brush and feed Sakura, our cat, and water my plants/sprouts. Today, I also folded the laundry and took out the trash to get some points with my partner (who does most of the household chores). Yet I've been cooking more. I made a weird, watery bean soup with fresh vegetables last night, and I cleaned the upstairs toilet, and gave her a shoulder massage last night. (My partner, not the toilet, of course!) So, I'm trying to be clean and neat in our small space, and talk less, and listen more. Not easy to do, but I'm trying.

I did my dancing outside after our walk this morning, and it was good to get out the kinks in my shoulders, hips, knees, neck, ankles, etc. But our two neighbors were on their phones the whole time; one was outside, and the other inside, with her sliding door open, so I heard everything at once while trying to do my happy dance. It made me angry and stressed, so I cut my happy dance short. I couldn't concentrate on me, my mind, my body, etc., with them obnoxiously blaring away into their receivers. He was talking about not being able to go to his usual coffee shop (inside), and she was talking about all those protests we're seeing on the news.

I'd imagine she's the type of self-centered protester who wants to open up the beaches, trails, and businesses so everyone can get sick—they think that's okay. These greedy people protested downtown on Saturday, and at the beach, not far from us. They're out there to be selfish and basically kill off everyone, especially those who are vulnerable, and the rest of us who are obeying the stay-at-home order, like good citizens, and not complaining to the world about it. Geez. I'll try to do my happy dance later, after my classes, if I get a chance. Until then, I'll try to keep on breathing!

April 21st, 2020, Tuesday, Day 43

I really am planning to paint, draw, and/or color my sketches in my dance sketchbook sometime soon. I'd like to blow them up, though, so I can have more space on the page. I'm quite a perfectionist, and I wouldn't want the colors to bleed into the black part, or worse, into the next segment of the drawing. It reminds me of my first real job in San Francisco. I got it right when I moved there, when I was in my early twenties. I was hired as a cartoonist, but I was never paid for my cartoons. Instead, I just got meal vouchers, so I received some tasty food, but no money. I had to stop because it wasn't sustainable. I'm not making any money on these drawings either, of course. And I'm not getting any meal vouchers, either. I haven't got a publisher yet, or an agent, or readership, but I hope to remedy all that really soon.

Before I do the coloring, however, I need to keep drawing and writing, and I don't think this dance research/dance journal/sketchbook can end until the coronavirus stops, and we're all let out of our cages. This project was supposed to stop with the end of our course, which is over in three weeks, but now I think it will continue through summer, when, hopefully, we'll all be able to go back to our daily lives and go outside, work, shop, congregate, eat, drink, do sports at the beach, hike trails (even though I hate the 'h' word), etc., and not necessarily in that order.

I'm so behind on so many things, and there's still all the other stuff I have on my 'to-do list' every day. But at least I'm learning a very important survival skill out here in this closed-off, shelter-in-place jungle of no rules—and too many rules… I'm learning to unwind, unravel, prioritize me and my health, my sleep, my nutrition, my family, certain close friends, students, nature, etc. *That* I'm learning to do, even if I'm not doing 80% of what's on my to-do list every day.

Before COVID-19 and this sudden pandemic, I achieved 80% of my to-do list each day. My stress levels were 80% higher, too. And before last year, I'd say, when I started this dance research in early March 2019, with 5Rhythms, I did 95% of the long assortment of things on my list every day. I slept four to five hours per night, I didn't listen to my body saying "Stop, that's enough!" I pushed, prodded, pulled, and forced myself to work until 10:00pm every evening, watched an hour of TV with my partner until 11:00pm, then collapsed in bed.

At 4:00am, or even earlier, I was back up, writing, reading, preparing, meditating, etc. So, I functioned on little sleep, little exercise, less interaction with my partner, family, friends, and kitty, and I was stressed out of my mind, even though I was teaching mindfulness, researching mindfulness, and how to achieve a successful work/life balance. I was also writing fiction, and presenting my books all over the place—go figure!—in addition to preparing all of my coursework.

That life is over. I've turned the page. I'm slowing down. I've learned my lesson about burning the candle at both ends. It's toxic. It's dangerous. It's addictive. And I'm going to continue on this slow path to freedom even when this pandemic is over. I hope these lessons learned will teach others how to do their happy dance every day and appreciate all there is, and the fullness and peace that comes from paying attention inside and outside each moment. Cause that's all we have, this very moment. The rest is empty air and nothingness. Another sip of tea, and I'm off to grade, prep, plan, edit, and post the week's work in my classes. Can't wait for that all to end soon!

April 22, 2020, Wednesday, Day 44

I'm listening to a live stream program from New York City instead of participating in our usual dance class this morning via Zoom. It was really hard to listen and concentrate because the neighbor on the other side of our fence decided to fix an engine (his leaf blower, I think) for at least thirty minutes during this live program. Unfortunately, it made it nearly impossible for me to concentrate on the presenters.

It's nice to hear artists, dancers, and writers, who know each other so well, share their experiences, thoughts, and love on an online platform. I can hear their voices as they talk about their thoughts and ideas about this moment in time. It's a really difficult moment because New York has been the hardest hit by the coronavirus so far in the USA. So many people are infected and flooding the hospitals, and lots are dying.

One of the presenters said that it's been comforting, having the voices washing over them. One said he's feeling full, and even 'juicy,' and that's cool. Everyone can continue to work, and share, and be part of this process. One asked, "How are you dreaming?" I'm interested to know their responses.

One was not able to dream in real life or even sleep in a while. He said it was like waking up into a nightmare from which he couldn't find any escape. It haunted him. But now, feeling the connection and possibility that exists, he hopes it creates a portal to 'arrive.' Another is also sleeping badly; it's a twisted, awful dream right now, he says. He's trying to accept reality. This 'chameleonic proposal,' as they call it, helps them accept what's going on.

They're angry, trying to find peace in this moment, but there is less peace than they would like. They experience disappointment and anger. Sleep is terrible for another, but it's as if she's right in the middle of a dream. The others aren't doing as well in this dream space, wearing masks. She said, "Fear of that social contact being violated in the dream space… working with new realities and new expectations." Another said, "Finding a kind of refuge and practice… creating a new proposal for dreaming, a new possibility, inside the complexity of this moment."

One mentioned "Having agnostic prayers… and dreaming about hugging people… reestablishing and maintaining relationships." Then they said, "Dealing with practices of the world crisis, feeling the need to be with other people… and disappointment at how others are messing this up in the world." Apparently, dreams provide a sense of refuge. "Getting to the dreamworld is the difficult part. Sleep is not restful." One of the presenters said he's feeling fatigued because of so much uncertainty about relationships and loss on a daily basis. He described the very real possibility of tragedy, and he's wanting to look at his phone all the time because of this.

Another said, "Am I being the right kind of human? Art practice has at least allowed me the space to breathe. It's the place where we can be, too, including dance, writing, etc. Where we can see, can find refuge in the midst of this ongoing crisis."

I can't see who is talking when each of them is speaking through YouTube. I can guess, but I'm not entirely sure. "There's an urgency to find rest whenever and wherever we can. If our creative process gives us a chance to rest, then so be it." That was Jaamil, I think. This stuff is really interesting. "The desire to practice love is what keeps me motivated. I have to remember that 'hope is a discipline.'" Apparently, Marianne K. said this. And Ashon C. added, "It's something we have to practice. It's a disposition, a method to engage the world, and it's so urgent in a time like this."

This is called "the dialogue channel." I wonder how many people are on this live stream, which I'm watching via YouTube live. It's quite interesting, I must say, to hear all of this and be in my living room safe in California, sipping tea at the same time. I'm loving this opportunity to hear them share and converse, since Jean has asked us to take notes and reflect on this program today. Especially now that my stupid neighbor has stopped his mega-loud machine, I can finally be present with everyone.

Here's a question from an audience member asking about "instances of surprise and improvisation in the work that they do." It's a good question. According to Ashon C.: "It caused me to do it, and not the other way around. I'm a vessel or conduit to do it. It finds me and helps me to materialize the thing. I don't find it; it finds me, whether I'm writing or dancing. It's humbling to me the way the work continues to allow me to be used in its materialization. Writing about loneliness isn't fun; it's born about of frustration and deep longing. It's never easy or frivolous, and I'm always surprised and thankful for that, too."

This comes from Nae: "It's working with alchemal attuning." That's a really cool statement. "Opening a portal through which these ancestral fluencies can flow through." I have discovered "Little Brown Language," which is quite an interesting project.

Nae started with a tarot reading to work with embodied and intuitive practices in a mystical kind of way. "Cut through the bullshit," said the tarot reading. The sword was the symbol of thoughts, harnessing clarity, bringing courage, too. Creative courage. "Artists are that future-looking symbol, reflecting back to our world what we can see, often beyond that bullshit going on around us... What can you build and channel in fifteen minutes each morning to activate that alchemy of the moment in spontaneous ways to shift and activate those energies?" Really, really cool advice!!! "Build, channel, and activate."

Another inspiring speaker said: "Offering a space to reflect; seeing the changes in spring plants and nature, teeming with life. That's inspiring to see the ways these plants and geese are going out, as we humans go in. How the earth changes as we feel the catastrophe for us, but it's still happening, and it's humbling. The time of these minute changes that exist outside my watch, on my walks outside, seeing all these emergences that happened despite our lockdown inspires me. And I feel grateful for that."

The live stream will end soon, and then the closing music will begin. It's the beginning of a conversation. This has been a really enlightening experience. Luckily, our class decided to listen to these great artists, who are willing to share their thoughts to shape our future by 'leaning into that reality.' This is a cool way to end the program. I took two pictures of the screen to prove to Jean that I was there. Until tomorrow!

THURSDAY — CALM
TRYING TO STAY CALM DESPITE UNCERTAINTY
SLEPT BADLY.
NYC + NJ NEWS VERY DISTRESSING
COOLING TODAY

Day 45

LONGER, WILD HAIR

SUNNY DAY

MASK OUTSIDE

OUR CAT VOMITED LAST NIGHT +

RICE + SOAK BEANS (FAVAS) ???

TO TAKE TO MOM TOMORROW

NEIGHBORS CAN SEE ME + I DON'T GIVE A ——!

OUR BIRDIE'S NEST IS EMPTY (SAD TIME) PREGNANT DOVE GONE (HER MATE CAN'T FIND HER)

DANCING OUTSIDE IN PATIO (GETTING OUT KINKS IN BODY)

CRACKED EGG SHELL

OUTSIDE IN PATIO

Day 46

HAPPY DANCE

TRANSFORMING MY EXPERIENCE W/ SOUNDS. ANNOYING NEIGHBOR'S CHATTER IN LOUD VOICE → INTERESTING DIALOGUE CURIOSITY + CALMNESS TAKE OVER!

80°F HOT + SWEATY

NEIGHBOR'S OPEN-SCREEN SOUNDS

WHY WAS I GETTING SO WORKED UP?

THAT'S ACTUALLY FUNNY

I LIKE OATMEAL TOO

I COULD BE HIM WORSE RIGHT NOW

JUST ANOTHER HUMAN EXPERIENCE,

"Hey, LOOKS LIKE SOMEBODY LIKES MY OATMEAL..."

"YOU KNOW, WE COULD HAVE PIZZA TONIGHT. CAN YOU ORDER IT ONLINE OR DO YOU NEED TO DOWNLOAD THE APP?"

"MOM, WHY DON'T YOU JUST CALL 'EM?!"

Sketchbook, Days 45 to 48

April 23rd, 2020, Thursday, Day 45

Today is a sad day because we can't find our little pair of doves that took over our hanging planter outside to make a nest and have their family. We've been watching them intently and lovingly for about a week, and today we discovered the tiny nest was empty. Then I found a cracked, miniscule eggshell on the ground with nothing in it. We saw the male dove and heard his usual squeak this morning, returning to the nest, then leaving again. And now, a few hours later, he's gone.

I've been playing soothing piano music all morning on my iPad and it has birds singing in it. I keep thinking it's our friends, the pair of doves, one so pregnant she might burst each time she hovers over the fence, her huge belly straddling it on both sides. But now they're gone, and I could only find an empty nest with little strands of straw-like stuff in it.

I picked up the half-shell and threw it away, and reflected on how Sakura, our kitty, was outside last night without our knowing it, until she came in and threw up all over the place. It was a pale, pink-color liquid, which I cleaned up on the stairs, inside my slippers, and on the floor.

We figured she'd eaten some scratchy plant leaves, as usual, and that the pink came from blood drops mixed with her saliva and gastric juices. But now, she's fine, and sleeping on the stairs above me, listening to the piano and bird sounds. I'm looking out at the empty planter hanging outside and thinking about the eggshell that looked licked-clean, and I'm wondering 1) did a big scary bird attack the mother dove and steal her eggs? 2) Did the mother dove die or get sick during her egg laying?

There hadn't been eggs yesterday, as far as I know, and I was watching the mother dove eye-to-eye, at about a foot apart, while I was trying to water the sprouts in our little planter, directly underneath her and her nest, as she sat there, not moving, staring into my amazed face with her dove eyes—and they really were dove eyes: soft, piercing, and so very real. Red, grey, and black... I'm not sure where and how all those colors went together, and a bit of white, too.

I've just never gotten so close to a wild bird before; it was transformative for me. Such a powerful moment, watching her raw beauty, being pregnant and protective of her nest—and whatever else might have lurked under her warm, soft feathers. And noticing both her vulnerability, and mine, as I wondered if she'd peck the heck out of my eyes as I stood there, facing her, mouth ajar in awe and admiration, clasping my watering can, trying not to shift under its heavy weight, pulling down my shoulder.

Now, she's gone; her mate is gone, and our kitty—who is elderly now, but has been known to kill birds in the past, unfortunately, in our garden in Belgium, without feeling any guilt or remorse—she's just lying on the carpet, lazy-like, lady-like, yet in her own tomboyish way, listening to me scribble in my journal. To her, it's just like every morning, I guess. She's absorbing the bird and piano sounds emanating from the iPad.

Sure, she might have been the culprit. I hate to say 'murderer,' because she's my little Sakura ('cherry tree,' in Japanese), and I love her so much, despite all that she's done in her life to torture birds, insects, and us, by meowing each morning at 5:00am so she can go outside and lick plants. Is she digesting the dove eggs and the little babies tucked inside right now? Or worse, is she digesting the mother? Did she just play with her innocent, bloated body, and then drag the corpse behind one of our bushy bushes?

I can't imagine this. I see the empty nest and think about the male dove who was looking for his mate, the mother of his offspring, and I hope they both find safety and peace, like I hope we all find safety and peace during this pandemic, which is killing so many people. I didn't write about dance today. I wrote about nature, and how it makes me feel. Vulnerable. In awe. Wordless. Not wordless, obviously. I'd say it's more like 'speechless.' Until tomorrow then...

Later today... I made a mistake. I was going to watch an online performance that we were supposed to watch for our class, and instead, I watched a video that made me tear up and feel so much grief, and deep emotion. My partner has just joined me for lunch, so I'll write about this tomorrow. I took lots of tiny notes on two post-its. It's amazing, transformational work. A happy accident, I guess. What a coincidence, right?

April 24th, 2020, Friday, Day 46

Yesterday, I was lucky enough to watch an online performance by a brilliant healer, dancer, and hospice nurse who presented their work in a large cathedral. They read about their experience about working with individuals who passed away in a hospice, which was really, really moving to me. They wrote beautiful passages about each dying patient; I found myself choking up with emotion, as if I knew each patient, too, and the patient's family.

It was like I was there in the hospice room with them, as they held the patient, looked into their eyes, and held the sacred space. I could see, hear, smell, and *feel* this experience with each written passage, as if I were in the cathedral with them. Then the images of them dancing, moving, singing, etc., were projected on a huge screen behind them. I was mesmerized.

This video was recorded before the pandemic hit. Theirs was a somatic practice, not a performance practice—a release of grief—and I felt that release of grief as I witnessed their testimony to each individual's passing, their tender and loving tribute to their transition, and letting go of their life on this earth, as if I were one of their closest of kin. It was amazing. I'd never experienced anything like this before. My entire worldview has burst.

The whole time I've been writing in this journal, I've been wondering why I'm extremely drawn to doing this somatic/dance research. It's like I'm drawn into a hole that keeps getting wider and wider. Instead of safely leaving it be and moving on, I'm creeping towards it, and at times, jumping in, not knowing what I'll find on the journey inside, which I imagine is the journey inside myself, inside the deepest layers of my soul.

It penetrates all truth as I know it so far—intellectual, physical, mental, emotional, etc., so I guess I could say it's like my body is now leaking human truths, a form of deeper consciousness that seeps into my awareness. It's always been there, but I've never taken the time to notice it before conducting this somatic/dance research (by doing the happy dance every day, reading articles, dancing with Jean's class and my 5Rhythms classes, and watching videos, lectures, and performances about dance). And it's kind of taken over my life.

It makes me wonder. My grandmother and aunt both became psychologists and their research for their Ph.D. and Master's degrees had a lot to do with movement, I believe. It's too late to ask my grandmother about this because she passed away fourteen years ago, although I always feel her presence with me, supporting me. Though I could read her dissertation, because I have a copy, but I haven't read it yet.

I could also ask my aunt about this dance research. She was a modern dancer but now she sees patients instead. She's the one who made me promise I wouldn't take this contact improvisation class because it would be too dangerous for me. But I broke my promise and took it, didn't I? She also told me not to move to a certain city in Europe because she had moved there and regretted it. But I did anyway and didn't regret it at all. I love her dearly, yet I rarely follow her advice, it seems! Maybe I'll just figure this all out on my own.

This journal I bought secondhand because I go through journals really quickly. I just realized there are a few pages missing at the beginning, and in the middle, right here. I wonder what the previous owner had written on them? I'm so curious sometimes. This could be a new story. Anyway, now I'm going to tune into a virtual conversation by women about the impact of slowing down during the pandemic.

I listened to thirty minutes of the recording, and now I'm going to listen to the rest. It's mind blowing! I took two pages of notes already. I'm not sure what I'll do with these notes, if I'll incorporate them into this journal, like I did after yesterday's performance, but I've learned so much already from these women, their experiences, and insight living in New York City as Black women, dancers, and writers.

They are very informed and thoughtful speakers about a range of subjects. The picture they put up on the recording included a gathering of Black women writers in 1977, wearing coats in a hallway at someone's home in New York City. It showed Toni Morrison and Alice Walker, two of my favorites. Wow! What an experience to listen to these women share their thoughts about the pandemic, the concepts of slowness, gatherings, social injustice, capitalism, etc. There was so much information that—as a white woman with white privilege—I've never even considered before.

Here are my notes from April 24th, 2020, from the Danspace Project in New York City on "Slowness." I've used quotes to record some of the most important information. Unfortunately, I don't know exactly whose words they are. It was a collective effort, and the presenters were remarkable. Little did I know that a little over a month later, their words would resonate everywhere in the world with a reinforcement of the Black Lives Matter movement, when so many people would take to the streets to protest for all the injustice that they've been subjected to. Maybe they knew this already? Their words seem to say so. The following passages are bits and pieces of what I picked up from their recorded conversation. Some of it might not make sense, but I wrote it down anyway, because I think it's really powerful. Here are some excerpts:

"The slow walk—make a song together, a song of dissonance." "Trying to reconcile this, the non-stopness… and the slowdownness…" "Do not stop, stop, shelter-in-place." "Who is essential and who is expendable?" "Slowness—of generating an intense perception." "Mobilizing slowness… micro-perception of slowness." "I'm trying to hold myself together here."

They were talking about slowness—being able to pay attention, and the desire to create space and time. "When you're an artist you want to get to this place… to work, where you can go 'full out' and it's such a privilege to be able to create that space for yourself… create a space of slowness for yourself." For example, they mentioned the class division, and how devastated they felt about it. I do, too. "Slowness allows you the chance to marshal the resources that allow you to go full out." "How can I ethically go forward? I feel so complicit in this situation. Slowness doesn't have to be the goal." "Or to face all the s... we're having to face and go full out against it." "The power of shirking and striking." "Slowness as a bridge towards realizing a connection that will allow us to go full out." These were snippets of their conversation, mingled together, but so very powerful. On the other side of the United States I sat in my living room and listened to their plight, wishing somehow that things could be different. Hopefully, this pandemic will make a difference in how people treat each other on our planet.

Back to my earlier notes in my journal: When I did my happy dance just now after flailing my arms and legs around for five minutes, like I always do, to sort out the kinks... and I heard that grating voice coming from our neighbor, and her beehive of kids' responses, I was filled with calm, peaceful awareness, and curiosity. I actually felt amused, and even privileged to be hearing so clearly her statements about oatmeal, her suggestions on how to freeze it, and eat it later as bars. (These suggestions weren't for me, but for the kid who ate her oatmeal this morning for breakfast.)

I thought about how we both, or all three of us, I guess, share a liking of oatmeal, but I bet they eat the sweet kind, unlike me, since she's proposing to eat it in bars.

I guess it all comes down to common humanity, curiosity, and amusement. Calm, peace, clarity. No thoughts of invasion of privacy (my own ears being penetrated by her stream-of-consciousness yelling), as I normally perceive her words. Instead, I felt at peace and actually privileged to hear so much, so clearly. For once, I put myself in her place and in her kids' place, with my eyes closed, standing erect on the other side of our wooden fence, which has dry rot at the bottom. It's frayed, but nobody's proposing to fix it since, I assume, we're all on budgets, especially now. There are one-centimeter gaps between the lime-green planks, and I imagine they can see me dancing, or standing immobile, behind our potato tree's thin branches each morning.

But I don't care; I really don't. It's our space, that's theirs, and we share it—whether we want to, or not. Why haven't I found this amusing before? Why did it all sound so muffled? And now her words are entering my ears like arrows—straight to their target—even though she probably doesn't know they're aimed at me, too.

Next, she proposed pizza for dinner and asked her daughter to either download the app or order it on her computer. Her daughter asked her, "Why don't you just call instead?" I waited for her negative answer, which came right away. It's like a ping-pong match, really. I'm the silent observer, eyes closed, standing there, absorbing this theatrical dialogue. I feel like I'm in a play.

I'm not the central element—they're the actors—I'm just the witness, the silent watcher, who has no ticket, no seat, no popcorn, with thoughts of "Why haven't I felt so light like this before?" I don't feel guilty at spying. Spying comes with the eyes open, like a peeping Tom, between the gaps in the fence, or else merely listening. And judging, of course. I was judging the quality and lack of substance of their conversation. But don't we all judge, whether we know it, or not?

Somehow, I felt a sense of relief. We can get through this. Yes, we can. All of us. I hate to say it, but I did have a thought… a very naughty thought that I'm embarrassed to admit, but I'm telling everything to this dance journal with authenticity and honest awareness, so I might as well spill it. I sort of imagined them all getting sick from ordering out all the time.

The daughter said later, "Mom, are you cooking? You never cook!" which confirmed my suspicion that they order out every day, or barbecue. Our bedroom was so smoky last night, I thought I was on the grill! And then, now I feel guilty. I imagined them all lying sick in bed afterwards, so they'd shut up and let us live in peace for a few days. Then I felt remorse at my bad wishes.

That's why I won't even mention what happened in second grade when I was sitting on the bench and wished a bad omen on the girl who stole my place as shortstop on my softball team—it worked! I felt horrible for years after that, after her finger snapped at the next ball. She tried to catch it, and it made this horrible snapping noise when it broke. I winced and couldn't look at her. Sure, I got my place back as shortstop, but I felt awful knowing the power of

Laura Kline

negative thinking—so I guess I *did* mention it after all. See, I do tell everything to this journal. It's dangerous! But amusing, too, especially in these lockdown times of anxiety and fear. I need a creative outlet, and I'm sure the neighbors do, too!

April 25th, 2020, Saturday, Day 47

It's sweltering. I'm sitting outside, sweating up a lake (cliché). It's 82 degrees Fahrenheit in the shade. We put our parasols up in the patio this morning, propped our cushions on the fake wicker patio set, moved some plants around, and hung a rug and a ratty tablecloth on the fence to hide the gaps between the neighbors and us. This morning, the noisy neighbors took down the screen that was between us and them, so now we can see their mattress outside on the ground and hear a guy inside making shelves with a drill.

A bee just got caught in a spiderweb not far from me and Sakura, our cat. She's very hot, with all her fur, but she finally stopped meowing enough to relax on the rug and watch the bee spinning in its spiderweb. It's making a zzzz noise and it's lying on its back, legs in the air, in survival mode. Reminds me of some of our moves in contact improv, but unlike us, this bee will not win.

I made a delicious soup this morning with fresh vegetables and my Indian spices and white fava beans that I sprouted for a few days. I slipped with the curcuma, however, so it's a lot spicier and bitter than I intended. Adding a bit of coconut milk softened the taste, and I know the curcuma is good for lowering blood pressure and fighting inflammation, so the soup should be good to eat, even though.

I've been cooking up a storm lately with the few, healthy ingredients that we can get during this pandemic. I made a super healthy kale salad with about thirty ingredients in it—I'm not kidding—and we took it and some soup, rice, and homemade banana bread to my mom yesterday. Honestly, I think she preferred the tuna salad sandwich from the week before, but I made it specially for her, to make sure she was getting enough fresh vegetables.

Then we went on a little walk and I figured out she might need more vitamin B12 because the soles of her feet hurt. That happens to people with white hair, blue eyes, and a lack of vitamin B12, apparently. I read an article about that once. She's not grumpy though, unlike my grandma, who had this problem and was super grumpy until she got a big dose of vitamin B12. And my dad needed regular shots of it, too. Despite those shots, he was often very angry. But I don't want to write about that right now.

It's really hot, I have lots of work to do for school, and I'm waiting for my Chair to ask me if I want to teach online, hybrid, or face-to-face classes in the Fall. I'm not sure what to say, and anyway, he hasn't asked me yet. And I still haven't finished my taxes!

My sprouts are steadily growing, and that's cool. And we're relaxing and taking time out to just 'be.' I want to meditate more, read lots of books, bike, draw, and paint, and I should post on my author website, Facebook, and Instagram, but I'm feeling lazy. And I need to call my brother to see if he's okay. I hope so. He lives in a nearby town and his roommate works at a large grocery store. It's not ideal, under the circumstances. We call each other once a week to make sure all is well. I've been doing that with my other brother, too, since the pandemic hit.

Oh, it's time to let Sakura in. She's upset and meowing at the drilling noise next door, and the blaring TV on the other side of the fence.

April 26, 2020, Sunday, Day 48

We went for a walk and then did our online 5Rhythms dance class today. Unfortunately, our teacher tried a new program and it didn't work for our sound system. Both our computers were playing the music, but it was like they were competing for attention, and there was an echo, so we couldn't hear our teacher's guidance. Instead, it was metallic sounding, like a boxed cage with music trapped inside. We kept on dancing, though, and couldn't really move that much on the rug without running into each other.

Our kitty finally woke up at the end. She watched us on the stairs and seemed to wonder what the heck we humans were up to with our caged music and weird gestures in the air. I was able to get out of my head for quite a while, except when the sunlight came in through the window and hit Sakura on her rusty, Calico fur. She had a white halo over her tiny head, and looked so angelic and beautiful, I got a sudden impulse to capture the moment.

Just as I was snapping a few shots with my phone, I heard Maya, our dance teacher, say to everyone, "Try not to get distracted as you dance to the music." Whoops, she caught me! I felt naughty, but it's a sort of delicious naughtiness, where you know you shouldn't have done something, but you couldn't help yourself. You were in the moment, and all hell could cut loose right afterwards, but in that very moment you'd rather do what you're compelled to do and suffer later. So, that's why I stopped dancing and took a few shots. I don't regret it!

Sakura's nearly seventeen and has already lost her sense of hearing and smell, and if she goes now—that halo was a bit spooky; I wondered if she was already ascending towards the clouds as I captured her angelic face—at least I'll have a souvenir of her beauty, calmness, and sweet soul.

Actually, I haven't been upstairs since this happened... We ate lunch and I decided to make myself a chai and write this all down, so for all I know, she's gone. Hopefully not, though, because she's such a wonderful pet and friend, and we need all the company we can get right now, since it's just the two of us and our weekly Zoom calls with classes, and a few friends. And our outdoor visit to my mom's house once a week.

I feel like I'm gaining weight and I don't know why. Maybe it's because it's so hot outside, but we're still trying to walk two to three times per day, and dance, etc. Maybe it's the chips and guacamole on weekends, and the red wine. But how do you have happy hour otherwise? Oh well. I did two-thirds of our weekly dance homework and have Nancy Stark Smith's video to watch and dance to later today, if I have time. There's more work for school to do, and then I can go for a walk and relax this evening. I might even make another pesto out of carrot tops if I have enough energy. Until tomorrow then!

FEELING OK. CALM.
I MEDITATED NICELY
TODAY

Day 49

SWEATY SUN → SWELTERING

HOT!

shorter hair
(I cut it. Looks good!)

SWEAT → DROPS — SO SWEATY + HOT

Doing happy dance
inside. Too hot
outside

HMM

DANCING OUTSIDE FIRST TO SHAKE OUT THE KINKS

SWEAT DROPLET FLYING!

MY PARTNER + KITTY WATCHING ME,
LAUGHING AT
MY SHAKY,
JERKY MOVES
(AS I DANCE FOR THE SPROUT)

DOING MY DANCE HOMEWORK

Day 50

DOING "MINI SOLO UNDER SCORE" — EMBODIED ACTIVITY W/ NANCY STARK SMITH VIDEO WENT REALLY FAST!

CLOUDY

A BIT AWKWARD

WHAT AM I DOING?

DOING THE ROLLING /
CONNECTING W/
AN OBJECT
(AN OBLONG
ROLLER)

HARD TO MOVE WITH THIS TECHNOLOGY!

EAR PLUGS CONNECTED TO iPAD

NANCY on MY iPAD

IMAGE TV 33!

LIKE A KID!

INTERESTING THOUGH!

FALLING BOOM!

DARING.

(IT'S BETTER IN PERSON)

OFF CHAIR?

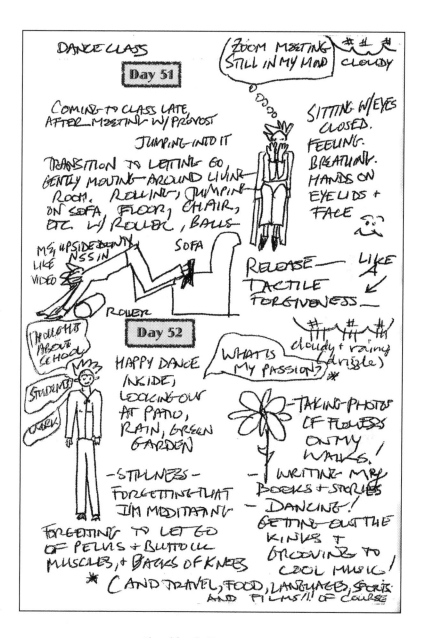

Sketchbook, Days 49 to 52

April 27th, 2020, Monday, Day 49

I'm sitting inside on the sofa with my second pot of tea, sweating the heck out of my T-shirt, shorts, and newly washed hair. It's hot outside—sweltering again. We went for a walk, as we always do now in the mornings, and we came back hot. Then I made some tea and danced out the kinks, as I do each day. After that, I came inside to do my happy dance, because the gardeners are back, making lots of noise with all their cutting, trimming, and clipping. They were gone for two weeks due to the non-essential-worker prohibition so there's a lot to do, I guess. Plus, it's super sweltering outside. My little sprouts are getting toasted and crispy yellow, which is not at all ideal.

The happy dance felt good to just stand there, close my eyes, and relax, letting gravity pull me down, connecting me to the earth, and grounding me. I tried to explain the experience to my mom last night on the phone, in vain. She didn't understand how I could dance without music and without moving my limbs. She asked, "Well, you're at least moving your facial muscles…" big pause, "aren't you?"

When I said, "No, I'm not moving any muscle on purpose, except for trying to relax my pelvis, the backs of my knees, etc.," she thought that was weird.

She said, "I'm sorry, it's just that I've never heard of this kind of dancing. What's it called again?"

"The small dance," I reminded her. I didn't mention that I'd renamed it the 'happy dance' or that this would most likely be the title of my book. She did think it was strange that I'm dedicating so much time and effort to do this 'non-dance,' as she hasn't called it, but she's surely thinking it every day. Or maybe not, because everyone seems to be having memory issues lately. Aren't we all, due to the pandemic and lack of contact?

Months of doing this happy dance, sketching it, writing about it, and ultimately turning it into a book. That's what I'm doing, while most 'sane' people are fretting about this pandemic and wondering whether they or their loved ones will get sick, and where their next paycheck is coming from. Hey, maybe this is all an escape? Perhaps my dance research and activities like this, recording it all down, is maybe a huge distraction from reality, because reality is too scary right now for me. So, it's a protective mechanism, learned in my childhood, to keep me from feeling the trauma of the real situation? To keep my head in the sand, so I don't actually realize or experience the horrors around me? I wonder.

It never dawned on me that this dance research, which has become a huge priority in my life this academic year, might be hiding the true essence of my reality, like the sunshade to protect my tender sprouts poking through the earth from the blasting sun. Wow, that's something that I'll have to think about. I've been considering this research, this process of going deeper, unveiling the many layers of the soma (body) and the soul, through a gentle, slow process of awareness, as heading towards the essence of life and reality—not the contrary.

It's not a shield, it's a gavel… No, what's that word, that thing, that tool you use to uncover the earth, to dig deeper? A gavel is what a judge uses to pound on the wooden block in the courtroom, isn't it? Living twenty-five years abroad taught me so many valuable things about life, but it didn't help me with my daily English vocabulary. I thought I had caught up, since we relocated eight years ago to the USA from Belgium, but I guess not. Gavel? Trowel? Who knows, and who cares, right? It's the essence that counts!

April 28th, 2020, Tuesday, Day 50

Today is day 50, so I guess that means I've been doing this contact improvisation dance research for fifty days, or more, because I didn't start writing in my journal every day until the pandemic started, when Jean gave us this task as part of our homework during the shelter-in-place order. I just finished doing the third part of our homework this week: watching and doing Nancy Stark Smith's "mini solo underscore" embodied activity on my iPad. It's 6:15am and I didn't want to wake up my partner, so I plugged in my headphones and tried to do all the movements that she asked viewers of her video to do in twenty minutes, but it was hard.

She started with breathing and awareness exercises, like I always do for my classes, too, but I noticed that she talked a lot about the body; of course, this is an embodied activity, which would have a lot to do with the body! I can't talk about the body or bodily sensations much in my classes because I'm afraid I might awaken my students' past trauma in their bodies. The classes that I teach on campus are not dance or mindfulness, so I have to be careful.

I thought of that while she did the breathing exercises; then she had us running around the room to warm up and get familiar with our surroundings. I was stuck with my iPad glued to my ears since the cord is short and I didn't want to ruin it. I tried running with it, but our living room is about ten feet by ten feet, which is really small, while watching Nancy on the screen and listening to her guidance. There was a large table and many chairs in the room she was in, which reminded me of our classrooms at school, and I wondered if she was filming this at Smith College since she's in Northampton, Massachusetts, and I spent a week at Smith last summer.

I'm feeling really nostalgic, actually, because I loved that week at Northampton, and I thought of this while I watched Nancy running, jumping, sliding, and slipping on the tabletop, the floor, etc. I wanted to be there to do it in person with her, not connected by a cord to my iPad, watching a fairly blurry image of her having fun while I was rooted to my technology—trying to be silent, trying to behave—while she was clearly enjoying herself.

Incidentally, I just found out that the summer institute, to which I had been accepted and even got a 50% access grant for, has been cancelled, and now it will be online. I'm going to tell the organizers today that I just can't participate online. I'd love to be there in person instead, but I can't. This exercise made me realize this, that I want to be in person for so many things, and right now, we can't—I can't—so I'm forgoing so many activities, conferences, and trips that I really enjoy doing to stay inside and "become a hermit," like my mom keeps saying.

Anyway, I watched Nancy slide off the table and onto a chair, and I knew she'd be a 'capon' ('rascal,' in Flemish, even though it's a type of hen). She was. She fell along with the chair onto the ground and landed on her butt, on purpose. Then she did a little roll, like it was nothing at all. Yeah, completely normal for a grown woman to come teetering, then crashing down onto the floor, directly on her backside. I knew I'd mess up my spine if that were me, and I bet she's was even born before me! Ouch!

Then she kept on going. She sure is a live wire. So, I took this as a cue to get off my butt and try something daring myself—within limits, that is. I don't have all her C.I. experience or bodily strength and flexibility. I took a big red roller that I've had for years and started rolling myself on its foam, cylindrical (is that a word?) surface, starting with my head, neck, back, and shoulders.

Then I fell off when I was on my shoulder and landed with a 'thud'; it didn't hurt and I didn't get injured, luckily, despite the fact that I was still attached to that stupid iPad, which limited my range of motion and playfulness. Somehow, I didn't wake up my partner with the 'thud,' and my cat scratched me as I tried to pet her afterwards, as if to say, "How old are you and what the heck do you think you're doing?" Now she's lying on my yoga mat, ready to take a nap and block me from doing further exercises today. She'd rather have her kibble, which is understandable, right?

The twenty minutes went by so fast; I have no idea how that happened. It was over almost as soon as the video started. It was a good virtual exercise, but I prefer classes in person, and I truly believe Jean's a really great teacher. I know she learned a lot from Nancy, so this was special, getting a chance to dance, play, and explore with her for a bit this morning, and reflect on the experience in my journal. What would I do without you, my trusty journal?

April 29th, 2020, Wednesday, Day 51

My eyes are so tired, dry, and scratchy, and my ears are ringing. I had four Zoom meetings today for school, with the Provost twice, and the President once, and over fifty emails with students, and then one hour of our second-to-last dance class with Jean. There were about nine of us in the class, including Jean, Susie, and me. I joined an hour late because of a very important Zoom meeting for lecturers with our Provost. I took plenty of notes so I could fill Jean in on what she missed, because she was busy teaching our class. I'm glad I went because I learned a lot, but boy, was I relieved to do some moving around on the ground, sofa, chair, etc., in dance class afterwards!

It was a rude transition to go from sitting at my desk, all stiff and proper-like, with glasses, a pen, and notebook, trying to ask intelligent questions and stay focused on the discussion, and then thirty seconds later, downstairs, joining the dance class via Zoom with Jean, seated in her chair, arms over her eyes, instructing us to breathe and feel the warmth and fullness of our hands on our skin, or something like that. She instructed us to feel from both the hands and face, eyelids and fingers, both ways.

It was so nice to take a somatic break. My eyes hurt, and my ears are ringing; I need to disconnect from all the positive ions, static electricity, and static body parts that I'm getting from sitting immobile for so long!

We have our new Heartbeat workshop with Maya, our 5Rhythms teacher, starting tonight in thirty minutes. I went for a walk, called my mom, who was out—and that's always a bad sign during this pandemic—and now, I ate two rice cakes with almond butter because I was starving. I'm often starving, lately.

I want to be silent and rest and just read or dance, but there's so much to do, it's incredible. And I've been frustrated with our Chair, who hardly communicates with us anymore. I'm so glad our Dean does because otherwise, I wouldn't know half of what's going on, on campus. Now, our Provost is speaking up, too. And tomorrow, our President will speak.

Well, it's time to relax before dance class. My partner is making banana bread that we'll take to my mom, along with soup, sandwiches, rice, etc., tomorrow. Yep, it's another day, tomorrow. I wonder what it'll bring?

April 30th, 2020, Thursday, Day 52

Today, I have a leaky pen. Ink got on my hand and my journal. I've been writing so much every day by hand, in both my regular, early-morning journal (in French), and in this dance journal, since the beginning of our contact improv course, that I've gone through at least twenty pens. It's cool because I'd hoarded a huge number of pens in a container on the kitchen counter, and only half are left. And I've gone through three notebooks since the pandemic started and I'm halfway through my next two—this one included.

Today is a grizzly, no, I mean drizzly day. I wonder why my mind said 'grizzly,' which is used to describe a bear, I believe, or perhaps tough meat, which I no longer eat? Or does it mean fatty meat? Anyway, it's drizzly and we're supposed to meet my mom for lunch, then take a walk around her neighborhood together.

I called her last night to tell her I'd talked to my brother. She talked a lot, and I listened and tried not to intervene, but she does some things sometimes that lack common sense and logic, and they could even be dangerous, so I had to say something. I don't think she realizes it, though. I'm not going to go into it here because I already did that in my private, early-morning journal, but it drives me crazy sometimes, and my partner gets agitated, too.

Anyway, yesterday after my fourth Zoom meeting, I had a fifth, and it was for the Heartbeat workshop with Maya, our 5Rhythms teacher. There were sixteen participants, including her partner and her. We danced and we learned quite a bit from her, which we talked about afterwards. She asked us what our passion was, and to dance with it through the 5Rhythms.

My passion was: 'the 5Rhythms, and writing about them, and dance, in my book.' Then she asked us if our passion had changed during the wave of music. Mine hadn't changed, and neither had my partner's, which was the ocean, although she saw and felt herself dancing with two dolphins during this red tide that we're experiencing, and its photoluminescence. All this while she was dancing with me in our small living room.

I was asked to work with another dancer, who has been doing 5Rhythms with Maya for a long time, I think—longer than us. My partner and I started doing 5Rhythms thirteen months ago, and it's transformed our lives. I guess I'll connect with the other dancer via phone or Zoom each week. My partner was paired with another dancer, and they're a really good match, too. None of the four of us wanted to be part of a group on social media for this Heartbeat workshop. The others will do that, and that's fine for them. I hate social media.

Actually, I have to force myself to get on Facebook. I do it very sporadically, and only because I'm an author, and it's important to have an image, a voice, etc.—a presence on social media. I get on Instagram now, too, also very sporadically. I just post photos of flowers, food, etc., with a comment below or above the photo—very short and a bit poetic, to keep people's interest. I always use my author pen name; that's why I didn't want to mix things up with my real name, which I'm using for 5Rhythms and our special Heartbeat workshop. Maya has also asked us to write in a journal during this six-week dance workshop, so this works perfectly.

Last night, I danced out my passion, but I kept yawning—I was super tired—and felt best when we got to *Lyrical*, after *Chaos*. During *Stillness*, the final rhythm, I stretched, instead of danced, to the slow, soft music, which was beautiful. I always feel torn because I want to keep dancing, but I'm afraid I'll pay for it later if I don't stretch right after dancing. I'm afraid I'll get sore muscles or, worse, injured.

During the evening, my partner and I both sweat a lot. Then we had a salad and a tortilla with a tiny bit of goat cheese for dinner. "Not enough," my mom said, but we weren't hungry. We did have some wine from one of our two remaining bottles and watched the second-to-last episode of a cool series on TV, after I talked to my mom.

I've decided I won't call her after dancing next week; having an intense conversation kind of lessens the experience—the afterglow—after being transported elsewhere through dance. It was as if we went to Mexico, since I think six of the dancers in our group are from there, and two are still living there right now. So cool!

I need to shower before my meeting today, so I'll end here. I hate the expression, 'killing two birds with one stone,' because I never, ever want to kill a bird again, or any other animal, not even a spider—and I won't—but that's what I had to do with Dad when I was really young, and then pluck the ducks for my family's dinner. But I wouldn't eat the poor birds, yuck! Not spiders, you don't pluck spiders, you step on them, and I did until I became a Buddhist, and felt the same as all living creatures on our planet. I no longer felt like I was more important than them, even if I'm a hundred times bigger and more powerful.

I'm digressing. Sorry. I'll change the expression to 'I'm doing two tasks in one,' by writing in my journal for both dance classes.

Next week is our last class with Jean, though, and I'm sad. I've only missed one hour of our course and I've always done the homework, up to now. That hour that I missed was yesterday, because I really needed to hear the Provost's words to us lecturers. I'll share that info with Jean as soon as she emails me back. Until tomorrow, then.

PS: the strawberries that I'm eating every day are making my lower lip swell. Too much vitamin C! But at least I'm sleeping like a baby (another cliché).

SLEPT BADLY 5 RHYTHMS   SUNDAY
LAST NIGHT
Day 55   Music

UP AT   SOFT, STILLNESS   everyone
3:38 am   AFTER FLOWING   on
again!   + LYRICAL (MY   completes
(too much   plugs→   FAVORITES). PUT ON EAR PLUGS
wine +   @ @ FOR CHAOS SONG—TOO
chips!)   METALLIC + GRATING ON MY
                     NERVES. (LOVING COMMUNITY
           MY PASSION? "DANCE MEDICINE"!)
                     ALL OVER WORLD
                     (GERMANY, MEXICO,
        DANCING IN SOCKS   SWITZERLAND)
        ON RUG — MUCH   SHOES OFF   Enjoy
        MORE FREEDOM!   being me
1ST DAY BEACH IS   Day 56
OPEN AT COAST   SAD SITUATION

EVEN   TRYING   NERVOUS, A BIT   Sunny
AT   TO AVOID   + SAD.
6 PM   PEOPLE   WHY ARE   SMELLY, PUTRID
       ON   THERE SO   AIR
       WALKS   MANY DEAD
       (w/o MASKS) FISH?   TAKING
                 RED TIDE?   PICTURES

       KEEP WALKING,   SWEATY + HOT
       M STANDING OR   BUT HAPPY TO
RED   STOPPING!   BE BACK AT
WINES   BEACH
    Seaweed   Dead fish   Dead fish
              curled up +   all over
              dry   beach

$\mathscr{M}$ay 1st, 2020, Friday, Day 53

Speaking of 'sleeping like a baby,' it didn't happen last night. About one or two times a week I wake up at around 4:00am—last night it was 3:45am—and I toss and turn and then I go downstairs to play with our kitty, who sleeps all the time. I brush her, or just scratch under her furry chin, and she purrs a lot. Then I make hot chocolate, without sugar, of course, and settle on the sofa to read one or two books that I'm enjoying. I sink into the stories, if I'm reading fiction, or into philosophy, if I'm reading something deeper. At the moment, I'm reading both kinds. They require a different kind of attention and discipline.

It's really hard to write while my partner is sitting down here in the living room and talking on the phone with her parents in French. I listen and hear what they're saying, and then I try to tune it out as I formulate my sentences while writing. I had the same issue today when trying to do my 'happy dance' (small dance) while hearing their conversation for forty-five minutes. I love my partner and my in-laws, but it's hard for me to multitask in the same room. I think it must be an ADHD thing—lack of filters to screen out the sounds while I'm working.

I just told my colleagues and editor in the UK that I don't want to be on a panel, or several, actually, that will be filmed and go on YouTube in early June after all. I've been presenting live at a well-known bookstore as a guest speaker/author for the past two years in the United Kingdom. And I was supposed to in June again this year, until the pandemic hit. I'd originally said "yes" to being filmed via Zoom, and today I realized that I really, really don't want people all over the world watching me in my bedroom while I talk about my books.

It's fine for my author colleagues to do this, but I use a pen name, like most of them, and I don't want to confuse myself, my students, my friends, and colleagues here by showing my face—I only have one face, after all, even if I have three names: the real one and two pseudonyms. This pandemic has helped me discover that I'm really a private person. How strange is that?

I've also discovered that this research for my next book will lead me to create two books: one written by me, with my real name, and one written by me again, with my other name. And if all goes well, they will come out at the same time. They're extremely different— one is a memoir kind of book about mindfulness, dance research, and slowing down (the 'Happy Dance'), which will be my authentic story during the pandemic. That's this book.

And the other will be the one I started three years ago, for which I have already written two-hundred and twenty-two pages. It's a work of fiction, even though some of it, especially concerning the main character, is autobiographical. It's a love story about two lesbian dancers from two diverse cultures, and once experiences symptoms of mental illness. It's also about dance, of course. I'm looking for an agent now, so that's why I don't want my face or voice plastered all over social media and the Internet. I want to keep working on myself from within, through my 'happy dance' and 5Rhythms research.

Now their conversation is over and it's time to finish my tea. Until mañana!

May 2nd, 2020, Saturday, Day 54

I'm sitting on the sofa, as usual, having tea and waiting for the delivery for our fresh vegetables. It's been coming in the middle of the night, so I got up at 6:38am to get it. But nothing was there. I keep opening the door to check, but nothing's there. We started getting this delivery around March 13th or so, when we stopped going out. That was also my last day at school.

Today, I'm not sure what happened. Maybe they couldn't get fresh produce from the farmers, or maybe too many people started using the service? My kitty wants to go outside because she sees her bowl of water out there. She keeps forgetting that we put another bowl inside, but she doesn't use it. I think she prefers blue to white. Oh, I can hear her licking behind me. She found it! Or else she caved in and is using the white bowl because she's thirsty.

We just went for a one-hour walk. We noticed that most people, including our neighbor whom we ran into on our walk, are not wearing masks, even though the law says that you have to if you go outside and come within six feet of someone else who doesn't live in your household. We had offered to get him a mask, and even put two of them, made by our friend, on his doorstep—one for him and one for his wife.

She was really happy to have hers, but she returned his because she said it wouldn't be used and that we should give it to someone else. I told him, "You know you're supposed to wear a mask outside," this morning, the second day of the new public order in California, and he replied, "I'm staying away from everybody and I'll take my chances." Then he walked away from us and we just shook our heads.

It's not like we're wearing them because we want to, or because it's fun. We're wearing them to 'flatten the curve' and because we're supposed to. We're doing it to protect people like him, who are older, and those with medical conditions. It frustrates us that so many people are careless and making light of this serious situation. It

Laura Kline

makes me almost not want to go outside and see others who are not respecting this rule.

There are protests all over the country incited by a certain person in the White House, and even people poisoning themselves by drinking cleaning products and rubbing alcohol because this person said on live TV that doing this could probably cure COVID-19. In fact, a student wrote me last night to apologize for not participating at all in our online class activities because she and her family are devastated by the loss of her uncle, who succumbed to COVID-19.

The delivery has just arrived and now we have fresh produce (leeks, asparagus, kale, romaine, radishes, etc.) for the week. Our kitty wondered what that 'thump' was outside. Her ears pricked. The eggs were on top and it's a miracle they didn't break. I keep thinking that things will slow down for me and I'll become more centered, and calmer. And I think it's happening, but it's hard to measure or compare with how I was before the pandemic.

I know I still have lots to do. My to-do list is so long every day. The difference is that I do about one-fourth to one-third of the items on the list every day, and most days, the only time I look at it is in the morning when I'm writing it. So, what is it doing to help me? I wonder. How's it helping me organize if I'm barely looking at it? Let's put it like this: if I didn't have one, I'd be so lost and behind. I'd get fired and so frustrated with myself for not doing anything, not knowing what to do, and when, not prioritizing… so at least I know I have objectives and things to do each day, even on weekends (today's Saturday, for example).

My long to-do list keeps me thinking that I'm getting things done because I add checkmarks in the evening if I did some onerous task or two. So, I guess I do look at it occasionally. And I feel good when I check off a task. But some days there are just so many things to do, and so little time. I'm feeling squeezed, like I've always felt before.

On other days, there's more room for play and creativity, and even ignoring my list—which I'm doing more and more of—preferring to read novels, or make tea and pet the cat, or watch the depressing news about COVID-19 with my partner on our iPad.

I have a webinar in the afternoon and have to post some things for school this morning. It's already 11:50am, so good luck with that! I think most of my students are *not* looking at my course online this morning, so I don't have to worry. But I do this each Saturday, opening up the next week's assignments, slides, and information for those who do like to plan ahead, because I'm a planner, and I'd appreciate that if I were taking my course.

My back muscles are tight, and I want to swim. I don't know if the beaches are open yet, but I don't want to risk braving the crowds on this hot, sunny Saturday, even if they are. Why don't our noisy neighbors flock to the beach today instead of yelling outside? We're literally camping next to them; it's crazy.

May 3rd, 2020, Sunday, Day 55

It's 3:45pm and we danced 5Rhythms this morning and afternoon, from 11:30 to 1:00pm. Then we ate lunch. I had my daily homemade soup, with beans, rice, and vegetables, and a bit of cheese, cilantro, lots of black pepper, and hot sauce. I'm now sipping a chai (which I make on Sundays) and sitting outside on one of our metallic folding chairs.

The palm trees are rustling above me and I'm using our new, tiny round table (purchased yesterday for $5 from neighbors down the street) for my chai and sketchbook. It's calm, for once, outside. The neighbors are eating inside, but now I hear lots of kids' voices in the parking lot, so I'm afraid they're back home, unfortunately.

It's nice to feel the wind on my skin, caressing it like soft fingertips. It's warm out here (70 degrees Fahrenheit), and my partner is lying on the sofa, watching me write. I wonder what she's thinking. She's often quiet, and today, she's even more quiet because she's tired. After lunch, we went on another long walk, like yesterday. It was at least an hour long. I'm hoping all this walking will help me lose weight. It should, right?

I need to work, call my mom, cook some rice, etc., but I'm tired, too. I got up at 3:38am again and had some hot cocoa, without sugar, of course, and sat with our kitty and read. I'm really enjoying that novel, and I'm especially amazed at the translation from German to English. I translated for twenty years as a profession and it's not easy to do literary translations. Of course, I don't have the original German manuscript, but I can imagine that it's magnificent as well.

A dog's barking, a motorcycle just roared by, and a lady across the street sneezed. I have ears that are more powerful than everyone else's. I hear everything, and it's sometimes a curse. I hear a distant radio; or is it a kid on TV? And an ant just crawled down the wall next to my shoulder. I plucked it off and put it safely on the ground at my feet. It smells like outdoors out here (makes sense), and I keep wondering when the palm fronds will land on me. They fall from our tree regularly, and there's a ripe branch right above my head. Luckily, we put up the red parasol last week, which should catch it before it can lop off my ears.

I tried to put passion into my dancing today by swinging and swiveling my hips. It was a lukewarm effort, but I guess I have to start with lukewarm before I can hit hot, right? I got mad at one song, in *Chaos*, which was metallic, yet slow, so I inserted my ear plugs and pretended I was bored. I was, so I just stood there in front of the screen (our 5Rhythms teacher can see us) and I did my small dance. It wasn't a happy dance this time. I felt my buttock muscles relaxing, the backs of my knees softening, and my feet planted firmly on the floor.

Our neighbor made a pork stew and salad for supper, apparently. She's still talking on the phone, explaining her whole dinner plans. Good, she's getting off. But now, our neighbor on the other side is greeting her sons, who just came home. And I learned that the pork-stew neighbor is eating supper at the lady with the doggies' house, and her husband is banging on something really hard to take something out, and I'm wondering if I'm going batty, sitting here, listening to him clamor and hit and do all of this just to piss us off.

It was quiet for about five minutes, and now everything's ruined. I guess this shelter-in-place thing is really getting on people's nerves—like mine. Maybe he'll hurt himself, banging like that. It's really annoying. I'm afraid his heart will give out one day. He dislikes us, and won't talk or even look at us, even if we say "hi" to him, which we still do, for some weird reason. He just sighed. Oh well, I'm going inside.

PARKS ARE OPEN NOW
WENT TO

Day 57

EMPTY PARK. NOBODY'S
THERE @ 10:30 AM.

SUNLIGHT
FILTERING TREES
THROUGH

WANT TO SIT ON BENCH + CONTEMPLATE
LIFE (MEDITATE) UNDER TREES,
LIKE BEFORE, BUT AFRAID OF
GETTING VIRUS SO I DON'T

PARK BENCH
← (EMPTY)

SO CALM
BEAUTIFUL
PEACEFUL

STAND + DO
HAPPY DANCE

SO
MUCH
WORK
TO DO AT HOME!!

OUR FAV CRITTERS!

Day 58

It's OUR LAST CLASS

Contact Improvisation

STEAMY

No music.
Only Jean's
great
guidance

SAD

NancyStark Smith passed
away on Friday. So sad.
What a shock! C.I.
trailblazer. Jean +
Susie's teacher.

Doing some
moving
so
that we can
stay round-
on yoga feeling
mat. gravity!
etc.

WATCHIN
NSS's
videos +
closing/
sharing
w/ all the
Class.

(18 participants) Class.

IT'S A NEW DAY, COMPASSION!

Day 59

+ AUDITORY

I'M A KINESTHETIC LEARNER

LISTENING ~ 3 STEAMY AGAIN

FEELING W/ BODY

ONLINE TEACHING WEBINAR ON ZOOM MY LAPTOP

DOING MOVES, FEELING MY MUSCLES + JOINTS AS I PAY ATTENTION TO SPEAKERS. LEARNING THROUGH MOVEMENT + STILLNESS

LEARNING A LOT ABOUT FOSTERING RESILIANCE

(THIS IS REALLY COOL, WHY DIDN'T I DO THIS EARLIER?)

JOINTS + MUSCLES LUBRICATED + HAPPY DANCE!

Day 60

IT WILL ALL WORK OUT!

TIME STOPS

DOING MY HAPPY DANCE IN OUR PATIO

REALIZING I'M HAPPY, I'M FULFILLED, I'M ENOUGH.

HOT! MY BRO'S BIRTHDAY

"CO-PARENTING IS HARD!"

BIRDS CHIRP

I HEAR HER COMPLAIN, BUT HER VOICE DOESN'T BOTHER ME. I FEEL THE SUN ON MY CHEEKS, WARMING THEM. MY HEART IS FULL. THIS IS WHERE I AM, AND WHERE I SHOULD BE.

(NEIGHBOR ON PHONE)

CARS WHIZZ BY

MY PARTNER HUGGED ME THIS MORNING AND DID 'NEUSKE NEUSKE' WITH ME, RUBBING OUR NOSES TOGETHER, LIKE ESKIMOS

"THE END."

Sketchbook, Days 57-60

May 5th, 2020, Tuesday, Day 57

I'll be honest. Yesterday, I planned to write in this dance journal. I even set it out by the sofa for hours, but I didn't do it. I taught all afternoon, from 12:30 to 5:15pm, and attended a webinar to learn online accessibility for teaching in the Fall. If we have to teach online, I might as well be prepared, but we don't know about that yet. And I did my office hours, but nobody showed up. Maybe the link is wrong, and nobody told me!

Anyway, after that, my voice was hoarse from yelling into the computer—my partner confirmed that yes, I do yell while I'm teaching via Zoom, and yes, I should get a headset. The neighbors will finally get some of their own medicine then, even through my closed bathroom window. Heck, maybe they'll learn something about my field of expertise!

My voice was hoarse after teaching three classes in a row, and then my hand hurt from using the mouse constantly during these sessions. So, we decided to go to the coast because the beach finally opened up, and it's a wide beach, so we thought we might not run into too many people at 6:00pm. Well, most people had masks on, which made me relieved and grateful, but some didn't, and some were even sitting or lying down, which you're not allowed to do.

You can only go to the beach to exercise—you have to keep walking, running, swimming, surfing, etc. And you must stay within six feet of people who don't live with you. Some people walked straight at us, like a group of four teenage boys who had just come out of the water. That pissed me off because they could've avoided us. Instead, we had to scramble like furious ants on the thick sand to get out of their way. That happened a few times.

Some people here just don't care about social distancing or wearing masks to protect others and themselves. My brother called last night and confirmed that he's not abiding by the mask rule when he goes out, except inside stores. I checked later and found out that the city he lives in has more lenient rules on mask wearing than where we live. I bet their curve of COVID-19 cases and deaths is higher, too.

It's been proven that masks are effective in preventing the spread of the virus, but he said he wasn't convinced. Neither is my mom. I didn't want to argue, especially since his birthday is coming up, and he's already received a big pay cut due to the pandemic, so I let it go.

I'm learning to let a lot go lately, especially my work, which I've always been on top of. Of course, I'm always there for my students, colleagues, and family, but I'll take twenty-four to forty-eight hours to respond to people outside this sphere, such as editors (my editor in the UK and a new one I just got yesterday for a story I wrote), and friends.

It seems like everyone is doing the same thing right now to preserve their sanity. We can't really go out and do what we normally do, or at least we shouldn't, so people are sleeping in more, doing less emails, and less cleaning—only the essentials, to keep going. That's what I'm doing, anyway. My priorities have shifted a lot since the start of this pandemic.

March 13th was my first day—that is, my last day outside with others—and so in eight days it will be two months that I've been sheltering in place with my partner and our kitty. By the way, the two doves came back yesterday! It was great to see them, and they came back again today! The mama dove is no longer pregnant, so I hope her offspring—including whatever was in the half-shell I found, which seemed like an aborted attempt at birth—are alive and well.

I'm going to make another fava bean soup today, and rice, and cut my partner's hair again. Then I'll do all of the work that's piling on my desk, literally piles, which I NEVER had before, such as creating the online final exams, paying my two credit card bills (yikes!), responding to well-meaning people's emails, etc. And I have a book proposal review for a publisher in the UK due by May 13th, and my TAXES (how embarrassing) are still sitting on my dresser in our bedroom (my office), ready to finish. Our accountant is going to hate us and it's all my fault.

They're talking about moving to phase two of the lifting of the shelter-in-place orders by this Friday already. I'm not sure if this is going to help lower the cases of COVID-19—I don't think so. They're doing it this week in Germany, France, and Belgium, too, and I'm afraid there will be a new spike over there as well. We'll see! Now, I need to get to my work and make that soup…

By the way, my happy dance was very still today, after our walk. I did it inside, and felt very still, and even calm. But my ears have been ringing so much more lately due to tinnitus. Either my blood pressure has dropped a lot, which it tends to do, or it's due to the stress and sound of my laptop speakers buzzing during all my Zoom meetings.

At least I'm getting enough sleep, even though I have nightmares again, which I haven't had in years. I guess I'm uncovering all that messy moss under the rocks in my life and it needs to be exposed to the sun and fresh air in order to flourish!

May 6, 2020, Wednesday, Day 58

We just had our last contact improvisation dance class with Jean today. It was sad to say goodbye to everyone. There were eighteen participants in our course, and that included me and, I believe, Jean and Susie. We found out that Nancy Stark Smith, who started the movement in C.I. for women—with the agreement of Steve Paxton, who created the contact improvisation form—passed away unexpectedly on Friday.

She had ovarian cancer and was sixty-eight years old and even taught a dance course at Smith College in March! Today's class was in tribute to her. She was an amazing C.I. teacher and mentor for both Jean and Susie, and she made the video in Northampton, Massachusetts, that Jean gave us for homework last week—the twenty-minute video that surprised me because she was so playful, bouncy, and taking lots of risks. I couldn't believe how she laughed as she fell 'smack' on the floor from a chair, on purpose, and then danced around the room, sliding down a table, etc.

We watched some videos of her when she was younger, at forty-two, I believe, or forty-eight. She was teaching students how to fly in the air, and the guy in the video caught her. Then she called the other dancers to her; they flew through the air and she skillfully caught them. We discovered that the crescent roll that we'd learned in class was useful since we can do it later by flying and wrapping our bodies around the neck of the person catching us and moving with us.

I'll write more later once I get a chance to digest what I learned in our last class. Our journals are due in a week and Jean will be giving us an extra assignment, which is also due in a week. I'll do that second assignment, which I believe is a reflection following Jean's prompts, and I'll submit a brief excerpt of my journal, with drawings in PDF form.

I'll tell Jean that my journals are going to be a book, and I'll let her have a copy of the manuscript, and Susie too, of course, once it's published. Or maybe I'll give it to them beforehand, to get their approval and feedback. It's such a great opportunity to be in Jean's C.I. course this semester. I'm so lucky that she's teaching it on our campus.

May 7th, 2020, Thursday, Day 59

It's a new day. I'm in an excited mood even though I'm sweating buckets after our daily morning walk up that huge hill near us, and after doing some movements, and then experiencing the stillness of my happy dance while letting my pot of tea steep on the sofa pouffe, or whatever it's called.

I'm in a good mood because I figured out that I can efficiently stand, stretch, and move while listening to webinars, Zoom meetings, etc., and not get bored or stiff, as I normally do. I usually can't stand sitting for twenty minutes or more, especially if we're supposed to dance afterwards, like last night's second Heartbeat workshop with Maya.

During these evening workshops we sit and discuss our fears and emotions and all I want to do is MOVE, with music, if possible, and not sit and share and grow stiff and sore in my joints. It creates a lot of inner conflict for me, and I bet I'm not alone in this, because she asks us to keep our videos on, and when I start to stretch or gyrate my hips, my partner says, "Do you really have to do that right now, in front of everybody?"

It's not like I'm looking for attention. I just need to keep my body interested in the moment, and what's happening, and I absorb things better when I can FEEL them. This applies to words, thoughts, and emotions—especially emotions, ideas, concepts, and imaginary pathways to higher consciousness, whatever that means.

I just write what comes to me in here and in my daily French journal and I have no idea what some of it means. I'm just a channel of expression, and of thoughts—hopefully, deep ones—and that's why I do this each day. It takes a lot of effort, time, and discipline to crank these words out on paper every single day, writing by hand, using up all the ink in my ballpoint pens, and doing my daily drawings, too.

This whole process takes imagination, creativity, trust, and guidance, but I do it because I know that these words that I'm writing right now will one day serve someone else, and hopefully lots of people, not just me. I know they have a purpose, just like I have a purpose on this earth, through this dance research, which I call my 'Happy Dance' research, and sketches.

As I write down all the thoughts that enter my mind and body each day, I hope I'll be able to publish something digestible, readable, and understandable. Boy, there are lots of extraneous words today. Where did these come from? Hopefully, this journal will even become popular, and it will be available in book and audiobook form for the world to appreciate. Even if it doesn't, and nobody reads it, I'm learning a lot in the process, that's for sure.

I'm sitting here sweating on my trusty sofa with my fiftieth, at least, ballpoint pen and fifty-eighth pot of tea (times two because I drink two pots in the morning, like all great writers, especially the British ones, right?) since we started this contact improvisation course in January.

It seems like so long ago when I entered the dance studio for the first time. I was really nervous. I only knew Susie, who came later, with Jean, and one of my former students, with whom I hadn't had a particularly close relationship, unfortunately. All of that changed... in a few short months. The whole group became so cohesive, close, caring, and all the rest—open, adventurous in a good way—and curious and aware. It's been an amazing, eye-opening and heart-opening experience, and I'm so grateful to Jean and Susie and the other students for accepting me with open arms, literally, into this contact improvisation course.

I took a whole lot of notes from my last session, but I haven't put them in here yet. We have an assignment due by next Wednesday, in addition to our journal, and I'll see how I can do that and still preserve the anonymity of these words; once again, I have no idea what that means, I'm just writing what comes to me.

A bit later: I ended up in urgent care just now because of a serious allergy problem and my doctor said I needed to go right away in case it was a mild anaphylactic attack. I then went to the pharmacy for allergy medicine. I popped a pink pill, took a shower, and now I'm continuing with my journal before my brain gets dizzy (one of the allergy medicine symptoms). There's still a lot to write down.

I made a virtual appointment with my editor in the UK next week to discuss my progress on my next novel (a romance between two lesbian dancers), and I'm not sure whether or not it's a good idea to share with her my news: that the more exciting and pressing book that I'm researching and writing right now is about my discovery of how dance, movement, etc., can make a person more present and in tune with oneself and the world through personal experience.

It's exciting because it's timely, especially during this period of uncertainty with shelter-in-place orders, when we are forced to look within ourselves for guidance and nurturing—and try not to freak out from fear and boredom. We're all enclosed between tight spaces—sometimes alone, often with others in the same household—and four walls. We're left to our own devices and creativity and protective mechanisms and we can choose whether or not to be led down that rabbit hole of fear due to the virus, sickness, claims that this is all a hoax, etc.

I chose—and I will choose for the rest of my days—to dance and write about this process and I want to share this experience with the world. It's another option at how to live, and I think it's a darn good one. It's healthy, safe (sometimes not, right shoulder?) and grounding, if it's done with the HAPPY DANCE in mind, body, and spirit!

PS: I'll put my notes in here maybe tomorrow when I'll be feeling more diligent and productive, hopefully. I have a book proposal review to write and submit today and final exams to finish writing.

Here are my notes from our last class: Nancy Stark Smith was a gymnast, and at age twenty-two, she approached Steve Paxton, the founder of C.I., to tell him she'd like to do C.I., too. He said she could. She was the first woman to practice it with him. Susie has worked with Steve, but not Jean. At the summer solstice each year, there's a Global Underscore in satellite clusters all over the world (Nancy created the Underscore) and this year, due to the pandemic, it will probably be virtual, according to Jean. It will be on Sunday, June 21,

2020. *That's today, actually, which is the day that I'm finally typing up these notes. What a coincidence!*

Nancy used to say, "steady practice," and "all in, all the time." In class, we watched a video on YouTube about Nancy Stark Smith. It was created by Jared Williams after her recent passing. She said in the video, "If I'm too tense, I don't feel gravity." That's interesting. She also said, "The earth's bigger than you, so you might as well coordinate with it." Interesting too!

These were her words, too: "Not too loose, and not already committed. In between." Also, "Negotiate these last six… How we negotiate them determines survival." I'm not sure I got the meaning of the 'last six,' however. Maybe it's the last six inches to the floor, where most injuries occur. And Nancy quoted Rimpoche, "Can we replace ambition with curiosity?" So cool! She always wore a long braid, even when dancing and flying through the air, and that's how people recognized her. "Practicing enoughness" was part of the practice. Everything that Jean has offered us in class had a part of "Nancyness" in it.

As I mentioned earlier, when Steve Paxton started contact improv in 1972, it was mainly for male dancers, until Nancy Stark Smith asked if she could join his group. She was so inspirational, even though I never got the chance to meet her in person. It's sad because I was supposed to go to Northampton again this August, like last August, for a summer session in a different academic field. I would've loved to meet her. She was always expressing such childlike exploration and wonder, with wide eyes and an amazing smile.

Incidentally, I really enjoyed watching her fall off her chair on purpose (see the drawings that I did in my sketchbook after I did her Underscore practice with her, in the video she recorded in Northampton, MA). I did that practice three days before her recent passing.

I could tell she was a great mentor and seasoned teacher to so many great dancers and teachers, including Jean and Susie. Her love of life while daring to explore so much through C.I., and her authenticity, really shows through in the videos and articles that she wrote for CQ (Contact Quarterly), the magazine she founded and edited for forty-five years.

"Contact jam—you recognize it as a language, even though it's not codified." "We transmit from body to body." These are some other things I heard during our last class. The last CQ (Contact Quarterly) print issue about C.I. was the Dec/Jan 2020 edition. Nancy Stark Smith started the magazine in 1975, and like I mentioned earlier, it has been published for forty-five years.

"How do we keep dancing?" she said, and then, "Throwing in the bouquet." She left a huge legacy. She was an elder dancer with "grounded buoyancy; unique readiness to rebound." "No petering out... The Underscore—it's a flight." She taught flying skills. "They're not wrong if you survive them." I believe she offered goodies to her fellow dancers: "Watermelon or chocolate... Sharing heightens the senses."

Malcom Manning also did the video.

Susie said, "Flying catches—terrifying—for some people not accessible—flying is exhilarating." Then she added, "The bounce back of compression is recovery."

In addition to CQ, there's Dance Magazine. At the end of class, Jean showed pictures of our peers from her former two C.I. classes at our university. They were really cool, and her students were doing some amazing contact improv moves.

May 8th, 2020, Friday, Day 60

Wow. I just realized that I'm done writing this first draft of my book, Happy Dance. This is my last official journal entry for the book, and for Jean's contact improv course. I've been pushing myself so much since the end of January, when this course started, and since March 13th, which was also a Friday, like today, when we stopped going to campus for classes.

I've been diligently drawing in my sketchbook, and doing my happy dance, and all the exercises, readings, reflections, and research that were required for this course, except for the fact that we couldn't do the C.I. jams that were planned on Monday nights downtown. I'm sad about that because these jams seemed dangerous yet exhilarating!

Moreover, we couldn't continue to dance together in person and try the leaping, flying, and falling, as planned, like Nancy Stark Smith did in her videos that Jean sent us. She also gave us a cool article about Nancy. I'll read it before I write my reflection, which is going to be our final project, in addition to submitting our journals. Both are due next Wednesday.

The reflection has about twenty-nine prompts, I swear. Jean has a huge imagination and I know she wants to get us to really reflect on how this course can benefit us and teach us about life, dance, C.I., ethics, perspective, proprioception, identity, justice, etc. It's great.

After I wrote her to see if I could just submit an excerpt of my dance journal—because it it's got sixty drawings and nearly two full notebooks of notes—and my final reflection, she said, "Sure," and I don't even have to do that, but I will. And she says she'll be happy to read my book manuscript (fiction) when it's ready, because I need to incorporate all the important dance aspects into the characters' lives.

One of the protagonists is a professional dancer, while the other mainly dances for exercise, and because she has ADHD and symptoms of Bipolar II, both undiagnosed… I didn't explain all this to Jean, of course, via email, and I didn't write to her about my *real* book, Happy Dance (this one right here). I was too chicken. But I'll show it to her and Susie—like my other, fictional book—when the manuscript is ready. And I'll send the book proposal to the person I've met several times already, whom I hope will become my literary agent… when the time is right.

Incidentally, I got Jean's response back during our meeting with our Dean via Zoom, and I was taking notes and worrying about how I was going to teach online in the Fall, as a lecturer, wondering if I'll be getting courses, or not, etc. I looked at my inbox and saw that Jean had written me to say that she's accepted a good tenure-track teaching job at another university!

I had to read her email twice to believe it. She's leaving in August. I'd been so sad for her about our abrupt tenure-track hiring freeze, due to the pandemic. She would've surely gotten that tenure-track teaching position at our university after so many years of diligently teaching our students and doing such a fantastic job.

Learning the news, all of a sudden, I felt sadness at my own precarious teaching situation and didn't want to continue listening to our Dean speak so kindly to us lecturers on the call. It suddenly didn't feel important anymore. Jean landed a great job after so many years of teaching as a lecturer, so I realized that maybe I could get one too, after all my years in the same situation.

Susie, her boss, must be devastated. If only I could teach dance—I could help her out! My partner and I started looking at universities after this. Once the pandemic is over, other good tenure-track positions will open up somewhere, where I will be valued more than I am here as an instructor, researcher, and writer. I certainly hope so.

I wasn't planning on ending this book (dance journal) today. Not at all. But my drawing this morning for Day 60 seemed like a perfect way to end it. I'm in peace. I'm feeling energized, optimistic, and confident. It's like a heavy load has been lifted from my shoulders and now I can sit back and dance forward! And write about all the transformative learning that I've experienced during this Spring

2020 pandemic, which seems far from over. But I'm happy to say, I'm in a good place, and now it's time to turn the page. Literally. To be continued in my next BOOK!!

THE END

Prologue

Final email to Jean, Tuesday, May 12, 2020

Hi Jean! I have decided to only answer the first prompt of your final reflection assignment for our contact improvisation dance class. I hope you don't mind. I've got to prepare for my three online final exams, which are all timed essay exams and start tomorrow. So, this is just a short snippet of my impressions of what I learned in our course. I figure you probably have so many entries to read, then grade, that you might be relieved to just get a page or so from me.

Please know that I have taken extensive notes from this dance research, largely thanks to your course, and put them in my dance journal, which comprises two written notebooks and one sketchbook. As I mentioned in my comments for the dance journal excerpt that I've just submitted, I combined my thoughts from practicing in your class and my weekly 5Rhythms dance class.

Lastly, as a reminder, all of these notes and sketches are part of my current dance research for my book manuscript, which I hope to share with you one day, when it's done. Once again, Jean, thanks so much for allowing me to take your amazing, transformative class. I'm so lucky to have been able to study with you for an entire semester, both in person and via Zoom. I wish you all the best in your future endeavors and I hope we can stay in touch.

With much gratitude and admiration for your student-centered teaching, and amazing dancing and choreographic talents, Laura

Final Reflection Assignment—My current definition of Contact Improvisation:

"Contact Improvisation is survival through unbounded experimentation; this practice calls upon heightened awareness of all of our human senses, including intuition; it unleashes extreme force at times, and combines the sensitivity and tenderness of feeling our body's core, muscles, bones, joints, the surface of our skin, from the bottoms of our feet to the top of our skull.

We sense the softness and fullness in an extreme state of being, either dropping into sweet peace or the uncomfortableness of stillness. Reaching the sweat of our efforts, through seamless—and sometimes jerky—movement as we connect radically with others in a loosely woven string of moments flowing through space.

Often exhilarating, sometimes dangerous, it's flirting with danger, the thrill of excitement, flying through the air, flipping, falling, being dropped, or caught. Snagged. What the hell is this? Every instant is different, every dancer is unique, with their own strengths and limitations.

This form unites and bonds individuals from all walks of life. It can ruffle their feathers and heal their wounds. Its expression requires constant practice, showing up, fostering temporal awareness, openness to different mind states, emotions, and feelings. We need to go inside, deep inside ourselves to really feel, understand, and know what makes us thrive. What is the particular rhythm feeding our soul? How can we define this passion inside, bursting to get out?

Contact Improvisation keeps us alive. It keeps us aware of our hearts beating in our chests, our blood racing through our veins. By daring to explore the physical and mental limits of ourselves and our partners, trusting that we will all become a bit more whole when we're done—after hours in the dance studio, in jam sessions, workshops, etc.—we may certainly be bruised, a bone or two might break, ligaments or clothes torn—but we do this because we know inside that we will emerge more solid and intact than ever before.

That's what I've learned about Contact Improvisation in this course. Dancers settle, move, jump, fly, soar, roll about the room. We explore FEELING, truly feeling, and absorbing new sensations—the texture of everyday materials: curtains, hardwood floors, rubber edges, carpet, pillows, even gym shorts, slippery sweat lining wrists, ankles, and foreheads.

It represents an exploration of bodies—together, and alone—in sacred silence. Sometimes we hear a wolf call, sometimes a yelp, sometimes we witness a tear, sliding down a hot cheek, due to pain, happiness, or the realization that we have just moved something inside; something blocked has shifted, opening up a stream of emotions that soothe us, unlocking the floodgates of our consciousness.

Dancing like this, exploring who we are in various surroundings, with practice and dedication, and quite a bit of nerve... who gives a damn who's watching us? We're digging down, reaching to touch our inner child, fostering our long-forgotten playfulness. By opening up to the universe, its smells, sounds, subtle movements, rotations, twists, and stretches, these efforts can give us a deep understanding of what it's like to be human.

In Contact Improvisation, dancers explore what it's like to stretch boundaries, what it's like to not only live with, but thrive inside our physical, round, spherical bodies, sharing space with other beings on a flat surface, or on sets of blocks, stages, sofas, etc. Yet we realize we're still on a round planet. Navigating this spatial awareness, this proprioception, at all times is vital.

If we're lucky—if we can remember to do this exercise for a few precious moments each day—we can practice the small dance, what I've secretly been calling the "happy dance"—and teach ourselves to feel the intensity and bloom of the present moment in all its forms. What helps ground us in these moments is noticing the constant pull of gravity, tethering our bodies through our pelvises, towards the center of the earth." – Laura Kline, May 12, 2020